SUCCESSFULLY DIFFERENT

An Alternative To Divorce

Arnie Wallace, Ph.D.
with Adryan Russ

CHALLENGER PRESS - **Solvang, California**

Successfully Different
An Alternative To Divorce

by
Arnie Wallace, Ph.D. *with Adryan Russ*

Special Thanks to Don Sorenson

CHALLENGER PRESS
Post Office Box 919
Solvang, California 93464

Publishers of

QUICK READ

Project Director: Marilyn White-Munn

Copyright © 1990 by Arnie Wallace, Ph.D. with Adryan Russ
Printed in the United States of America

Successfully Different by Arnie Wallace. Ph.D. with Adryan Russ
ISBN O-9625341-1-0
Library of Congress Catalog Card Number 89-82471

Additional Titles
Loving Tough. Loving Smart. Loving You © 1990
by Arnie Wallace.Ph.D. with Adryan Russ ISBN 0-9625341-0-2

Dedicated To

Ann

and

Jesse

Table of Contents

Table of Contents

The more than one million divorces in this country each year are America's testimony to an emotionally bankrupt population. Thousands of couples seek marriage and family counseling, but divorce is more often than not the way most resolve their differences. While I believe divorce sometimes is the best answer, I know there are couples for whom it is not. This book is for them.

Our survey of current how-to- books left us with the impression that many of them support and nurture the narcissistic attitude that the ideal life is a problem-free life. Life is not problem-free, it's not supposed to be.

My approach is no-nonsense, and, at the same time, is geared toward pointing out the humorous absurdity of our struggles. I believe being able to laugh at one's own imperfections is essential to learning and growing.

As an extension to previously published books on change and people's difficulties, *Successfully Different* offers human solutions to human problems.

Arnie Wallace, Ph.D.

1

THE JOURNEY

When we focus on our
differences, we wind up
with the exact opposite
of what we really want.

—The Paradox of Negative Focus

        My wife will not close the garage
door. I have asked her politely, kidded her,
scolded her, explained the risk of theft — nothing
works. For years, I chalked up her apparent
unwillingness to do this one task as a total disregard for my feelings. I spent hours, upset by her

indifference to my needs, trying to figure out a way to make her shut that door. I suffered every time I thought about it.

Today, when I see the garage door open, I walk over and close it. I'm much happier.

I know. Some of you are cringing. Others, scoffing. I hear you. You are saying, "You're crazy! You let her get the best of you!" The truth is, now she actually is getting the best of me, because the best of me understands *she* has no need to see that garage door shut. *I* do. Therefore, it's up to me to shut it.

I came to this solution by myself, without any coercion, without counseling. One day the thought simply struck me: I am making myself miserable over something that I cannot change — my wife's behavior. There is no way to "fix" her perspective, and there is no book that will tell me how to make her do something that she does not feel is important. I realized that to make myself happy, the only person I could change was me, and that the only action I could take to make myself happy was to physically go out and close the garage door.

Thousands of couples seek marriage and family counseling over problems such as this; even so, divorce has become the most common way of resolving differences. The more than one million divorces in this country each year are America's testimony to an emotionally bankrupt population. Quick-fix therapies and well-meaning tidbits of advice from friends and families are not reducing the number of broken homes. Our society has been promised short-term gains, our attention spans have been reduced to ten-minute segments between television commercials, and we have adopted the attitude that life should be easy. It's not easy. It's not going to be easy.

Many of us believe our differences are irreconcilable. The special people we chose as friends, the heroes and heroines we chose as partners — we have now labeled them *villains*. We say they've changed, or we've changed, and we focus on our differences. In my 25 years as a counselor and therapist, I've seen people sabotage themselves, their marriages and other relationships by insisting that people in their lives change, in a specific way, to fit their own needs.

What about you? Do you believe your partner should change? Surely the reasons

you fell in love with your partner in the first place
have not totally vanished. What's happened?
Remember when you first met your partner? You
may have been attracted by things you had in
common. However, I'm willing to bet that you
were attracted by something that was different
from you:

> "My God, he's actually on the Board
> of Directors of a Forbes 500 company!"

> "What a surprise! She travels every
> two weeks, and her job actually pays
> her to do it!"

> "Isn't it great that he grows his own
> vegetables in his back yard? Must
> save a fortune at the grocery store!"

Now, all of a sudden, those exciting
differences have turned into ugly problems:

> "If he didn't waste so many evenings
> at those Board meetings, we could
> have more time together."

> "If she didn't have to travel so often,
> the kids would feel like they have a
> mother."

"If he didn't spend weekends nurtur-
ing those damned vegetables,
maybe he could nurture me."

Perspective is everything. In a
Woody Allen movie, the female character complains that she and her lover have sex "all the
time: three times a week." The male character
says they "hardly have sex at all: three times a
week." We laugh at their difference, because it
is funny that two people can see the same circumstances so differently. If only we could see
our own differences with as much amusement!

Life is full of paradoxes. Every day
we make statements that contradict themselves,
and we take actions that get us the exact opposite of what we want. How we deal with these
apparent contradictions determines how we live
our lives. We can see them as frustrating and
painful, or we can look at them as humorous and
entertaining and learn from them. The choice is
ours.

Sometimes the best way to under-
stand the causes of our problems and find workable solutions is to take a 180° turn. In other words,
do the exact opposite of whatever you've been
doing that hasn't been working. For example, if

you've been wallowing in the pain of a frustrating situation, stop and look at the humorous side instead. I mean it! There *is* a humorous side; you have only to turn and find it.

In addition, if you've been doing everything in your power to get someone to do something, and he or she simply will not do it — stop. Just stop. Tell him, "It's okay — *I'll* walk the dog." Tell her, "*I'll* wash the car." Say it, and mean it. It's sometimes startling to discover what happens when you let go of an approach that doesn't work and make a decision to do the exact opposite of what's expected. Many of us don't realize that our problems continue to be problems because we continue to apply the same solutions. We get the notion that they didn't work the first time because we did something wrong. We don't consider that maybe what was wrong was the solution itself.

As you read this book, know that taking 180° turns and living with paradoxes are essential in resolving the conflicts that are keeping you and your partner from enjoying a healthy relationship. In order for you to make progress in resolving those conflicts, you will need to accept three factors:

(1) You are 50% of the problem;

(2) You are 50% of the solution; and

(3) Two conflicting opinions can be true at the same time.

Accept these, and you are on your way to making some important discoveries. I believe strongly that two people can be very different and still enjoy a happy, healthy relationship.

If you decide to travel further with me on this journey, I believe I can offer you a way to maintain and enhance love in your relationships as well as define a workable, ongoing strategy for dealing with your differences. I also want to encourage you to expand your sense of humor. All of this is, however, going to involve a willingness on your part to take three important steps:

(1) Get in touch with the core of your own true self;

(2) Look at the image of yourself you are projecting;

(3) Look at the world around you.

If you are not ready to do these things, put this book away. Give it to a friend.

I believe in a no-nonsense approach to therapy
— no wasting precious time and money. While
it's true that some people need long-term therapy, most of us can learn to deal with our issues
within a short period, provided we are willing.

The process in this book does not
take long to learn, and please remember, for the
process to work, you must use it on an ongoing
basis, as needed.

This is not a "Take two and call me in
the morning" approach. This is a life support
system — plug it in and make sure the electricity
continues to flow.

I assume you picked up this book
because you feel there are elements of your
relationship that leave you wanting — elements
you would like to change, if you could. For example, how many of the following apply to you?

If my partner would change, she/he
would be a better person.

I wish my partner were less competi-
tive. I always have to prove myself.

I'd like to be the way my partner

wants me to be, except that that
isn't me.

I enjoy being totally dependent
upon my partner.

I enjoy my partner being totally
dependent upon me.

If my partner would just do what I
say, we'd get along better.

If my partner got some therapy,
we'd be okay.

If my partner would just shut the
garage door, I could be a happy
person.

Fess up. Certainly one of these ap-
plies to you. Probably more than one. Every one
of them has been true for me at one time or
another. My family and I find our way through
one major crisis — and in no time we have a new
one on our hands. This is life.

Learning how to let go of our
struggles takes time and thought. It requires that
we focus on the truth that lies deep within us.

What is true for you may not be true for your partner. Sometimes when we find our own truth, we have difficulty staying with a partner with whom we have been living a lie. But finding the truth is the only way to go.

I want to help you discover the true you, because I feel it's time you knew your *self*. You have had to be too many other people in your life in order to survive. I know you want to genuinely love and be loved. I know you want to be able to relate to those you care about. And I know that deep down you want to be accepted for who you really are. I don't know anyone who does not want these things. That's why this book was written.

2

THE TRUE YOU

The more I try to prove
I am not selfish,
the less self I have.

—The Paradox of Self

At some point in time, each one of us entered this life as an exquisite, loving being. We were infants with no preconceived notions, no problems, no hang-ups; and in order to be the object of everyone's love and affection, all we had to do was *be.* It was a perfect existence.

Perhaps we were loved a little less when we cried than when we cooed; nevertheless we were loved for being who we were — drooling, diaper-wetting, eating and sleeping dependent little creatures who did exactly what we wanted.

As we got older, things changed. We learned to walk, which took us to places we could reach and things we could touch. We learned to talk, which helped us communicate our needs. With walking and talking, however, came rules, some of which taught us a major life lesson: Sometimes we must give up something in order to get something.

"If you want dessert, you'll have to clean your plate."

"Finish your homework before you watch television."

"You have a nasty temper. You better learn to control it, if you know what's good for you."

Perhaps you gave up toys, games, fun, money. Maybe you gave up time and energy. What you may not have noticed is that there were occasions when you gave up something less visible, yet far more essential to your well-being: your *self*.

First Messages

We got our first messages about who we are from our parents, family, teachers and friends. They all told us who they thought we were: "You're so pretty!" "You're a genius!" "You, young man, are nothing but trouble." For some of us, their vision of us was clear and their ability to accept us was free, so that what we felt and what they saw had some correlation. Many of us, however, were not that fortunate.

Anyone who has ever been two years old has gotten the message, at one time or another, that being yourself is going to get you in a lot of trouble. Invariably, this message came when being yourself included doing something that somebody bigger than you didn't go for. In some cases the people sending you messages were loving; in others, people were ill, confused, stuck in their own beliefs, or upset about other things. From time to time, you may have gotten mixed messages. For example, if your parents instructed you to believe in the beauty and sanctity of marriage, and fought every night, you may have gotten mixed up about what marriage is supposed to be.

When we're growing up, we are very impressionable. What we see and hear we take as truth. At some point in your life, you may have seen or heard the message that you were not acceptable as your self. Perhaps someone communicated that you were too loud, too fat, too short, too slow, too fast, whatever.

Maybe you met someone who didn't seem to like people who were "smart," so you made a decision, right there and then, to hide your intelligence. Maybe someone didn't like your self-assured attitude, and you decided, from that moment on, that you would never show self-assurance again. Perhaps you refused to do something you didn't want to do, and you were spanked or disapproved of by someone you loved. In that moment, you may have decided that expressing refusal was not safe. Sometimes a single message can last a lifetime.

All of us have gone through the experience of giving up pieces of our true selves. It's very much a part of being alive, and there's no question that it's also a kind of death.

What Have You Given Up?

Do you remember what you gave up to get what you wanted? I know, it was a long time ago. Maybe you're not sure you recall anything in particular. Maybe you're not interested in drumming up painful memories. What I ask is that you take a 180° turn and look upon these questions as an exercise in information-gathering. Scientists do it all the time. There is no *good*; there is no *bad* — there is only what *is*. Whatever you gave up simply *is*. Nobody has the right to judge you for the decision you made. You did what you had to do to take care of yourself.

The best way to begin this exercise is to look at little "things" about yourself that you don't particularly like. Then, see if you can remember where these dislikes came from. I'll go first to give you the general idea.

Every now and again, I tell myself I don't like the way I...

am in a hurry and want everyone else to be in a hurry to get things done. When they are not done, I become disappointed. This entitles me to get angry — very angry.

Where I think I got this behavior is...

from the expectations of adults
when I was growing up, that I should
hurry — get things done faster and
better than others. The premature
death of my father contributed to
this hurry-and-grow-up message. I
gave up being the little boy I was,
since I was not treated like one. I felt
a continual urgency to do more, be
more. If I dawdled, as kids do, I felt I
was doing something wrong. I developed impatience with myself and
others.

**The way I came to dislike this
characteristic in myself is...**

I noticed that people do not enjoy
working under the threat of anger. I
have a hard time keeping people
involved, interested and working efficiently when they feel strained by an
environment in which there is very
vocal anger.

By looking at traits I don't like about myself, I begin to remember criticisms I got from people. I recall those times I was asked to fit into somebody's preconceived notion of how a "good little boy" ought to be; then, as I got older, how a "man" should be: *We men should get things done quickly. People who are slow get in the way.* Those pieces of myself I gave up are part of the original *me* that died.

Okay, your turn. Take a few minutes to think about these statements, so that you complete them honestly.

Every now and again, I tell myself I don't like the way I...

Where I think I got this is...

The way I came to dislike this characteristic in myself is...

If you've come up with one or two of these, you're doing very well. If you're having trouble remembering right now, come back to this later. The point is that you've begun to think about it.

How Do You Know You've Been Giving Your Self Up?

We've become so good at covering over those times when we give our selves up, we often don't know we are doing it. Here's a common pattern of feelings that occurs:

— Someone asks you to, say, walk the dog tonight. You've had a long, hard day; you don't think it should be your job to walk the dog at midnight. However, you don't refuse. There is a numbing of feelings. You say, "Sure!" "No problem!" And you walk away. You don't feel good for a moment. You quickly wash that feeling away.

— You feel attacked without being able to hit back — an internal flinching similar to how a child feels when the class bully walks by. You may get a foggy memory — perhaps of when you were a kid and you were asked to stay home instead of going on a trip with friends, or a time you were

told to do something you didn't
want to do.

— This fear or dislike of something
  you're afraid to confront in-
  creases its numbing effect until
  there is very little feeling of aliveness. You don't feel right; you
  don't let yourself feel anything.

— Your aliveness gets bottled up
  deep inside. You don't let it out
  except in times of extreme emo-
  tion, when you uncontrollably
  explode like Mount St. Helen.

As adults we continue to give our
selves up because this is a behavior we learned
early, and no one has told us we don't have to
do it anymore. Guess what? You don't have to
do it anymore. You no longer have to defer to
anyone who takes you away from yourself, no
matter whether it's your mother, your father, a
boss, advertisers, politicians, doctors, lawyers or
Indian chiefs. You are no longer a child, and you
no longer need anyone to tell you what to eat,
wear, drive, buy; where to live, travel, shop; how
to look, feel, or be.

How Do You Get Your Self Back?

The road back may have many forks. The best path begins with becoming *aware* of your self, and becoming sensitive to the times when you are *not* being your self.

For starters, think of the times in your day when you play a role, become someone else, or put on a front. For example, you may put exhausting time and effort into being *the perfect spouse* or *the ideal executive*. Have there been times when you've found yourself in need of a human response and have been unable to get a satisfying one? Have you felt that you were getting a response to your image rather than to your *self*?

Do you think it's possible that the people in your life have not been responding to the *real* you, because you haven't *been* the real you?

Most of the approval we get in our lives is for doing; very few people know a feeling of approval for simply being. I know men who decide to *be* a jock instead of participating in some sport. I know women who decide to *be* a size 10 instead of doing healthy things for their bodies. When the stock market crashed in 1929, people jumped out the window because they identified totally with their money.

Who you are is your thoughts and feelings. One way to get your self back is to get in touch with your thoughts and feelings — become *aware* of them. When a feeling starts to come up, stop what you're doing for a moment — and just notice the feeling. Don't do anything about it. Just notice it. Is it anger? Is it joy? Is it fear? Sadness? Jealousy? Elation? Carry the following checklist with you — in your pocket, in your purse, in your mind. When a feeling comes up, pull out the checklist and answer the questions.

Feeling Checklist

What am I feeling?

Am I letting the feeling show? If not, why?

Is this a predominant feeling that happens every day?

When are the occasions this feeling shows up?

How does this feeling get here?

Who does this feeling remind me of?

What do I get out of this?

How does it make me feel to be this way?

What would happen if I weren't this way?

How have I not been myself today?

Economy of Self

We've all heard the addage: the more you give, the more you recéive. For some of us, that has been confusing information. Some of us got a mixed message about giving. In learning to give, we got confused between giving and giving up self.

It is not true that the more you give up *self*, the more you receive. When we give, we give to others, yet we keep our selves. We must know the limits of what we can give. We have only so much to give to our partners; so much to give to our children; so much for our parents; so much for our work. When we reach our limit, we stop, because we need to keep a reserve for our selves.

If we compromise these limits of our selves, we give ourselves *up* and deplete our reserves. There are always good reasons why we do this — we want to win someone's approval, someone's love — the end result, however, is that we do not get what we're after. What we get instead is tired, depleted, ill. If, for example, you are accused of not spending a fair amount of time with your children, and you give up precious *self* time to win your partner's love, you may be left with a feeling of sapped energy and resentment — feelings which are not going to win you love.

If you have been giving your self up rather than giving, it's time to take a 180° turn. If you are frugal with your self, you are going to feel more alive while expending less energy. People in your life are going to get more of you with a lot less contact. When you maintain as much of your self as you need, you are balanced. As a result, your ability to make contact with others is effortless. You get all kinds of benefits: an increased fondness for life, a greater delight in yourself, a deeper sense of humor with others, and you don't have to spend the rest of your life working on becoming okay — you're okay *now*.

The Fertile Void

In the process of turning loose of your images, your illusions, and all the you-shoulds

and you-got-tos — there is often a feeling of
emptiness, a loss of identity. Know that this feeling is natural and is simply a bridge you must
cross to get to the other side. This bridge takes
you to a new place — a fertile void — an empty
place from which to grow. You may find it frightening to confront that void when you first feel it.
The questions hit hard:

> What am I going to do now?
> Who am I?
> What am I going to be when I grow up?

But rather than run away, take the
180° turn and face the void, head on. It's new
potting soil, and you are a brand new seed. With
time, you will weed out old defenses and find
room for new ideas and new people. That void is
you, and as you fill it every day, one day at a
time, with something new, you have the opportunity to grow quite a garden.

We can only begin a journey by
starting from where we are. No matter who
you've been in the past, or who you've thought
you ought to be, begin by getting to know who
you are right now. Gather information. Pull out a
piece of paper and create two columns. In one
column write down something you know is *true* of

you. In another column, write down a way you have been that you feel is an *image* of you — rather than the real you. For example, here's mine:

The Real Me	**The Image of Me**
I like to write poetry	Clinical and scientific
A real pussycat	A man-eating lion
Soft and loving	Tough and uncaring
A nature lover	City slicker
I like to spend time alone, fishing	Sociable, outgoing
Football player	Company executive

Piece the puzzle together slowly. Give yourself time. Every time you think of a *real you* characteristic and an *image* characteristic, add it to the list. When you've gathered several *real you* traits, ask yourself if you've been living the *real you*. If not, the time has come to make some changes.

When you invest in yourself, the returns are great; you get a line of credit from people. They invest trust, friendship and intimacy in you, and want you to be around. Nothing can satisfy those who do not invest in themselves.

If you are a person who has been unable to find deep satisfaction, consider the possibility that you have not been true to your self.

When I look at my beliefs, I explore whether they might be based on misinformation about how to be in the world. I know that when life gets frustrating and confusing, and I become irritable, what works for me is going to a quiet, simple place where I can look at the origin of my problem. For some people, that's a half-hour jog around the neighborhood. For others, it's taking a weekend trip for a change of scenery. For me, it's going fishing.

Living A Lie For Someone Else

In my practice I have come across several individuals who became what their partners wanted them to become. One woman told me, "I thought that if I became what he wants me to be, he would never leave me. Now he's leaving." She no longer has her partner, and she no longer has her self. What she didn't realize was that in the process of becoming someone she didn't want to be — someone her husband said he wanted her to be — her resentment began to build. She hid her feelings, yet they were there. They showed up in how she thought and how she acted. She lost her individuality as well as her desire for cooperation. Furthermore, once she became someone he said he wanted her to be, she was no longer the person he was attracted to in the first place.

There is a commitment made when you decide to live with someone. If that was a lie to begin with, forget the lie and find the truth. If the commitment was based on truth, then there is a duty to yourself to rediscover that truth. It's time to stop making the marriage your focal point. What needs attention are the *individuals* in your marriage. Right now, this means you. It's time to go fishing.

The True You

3

GAMES, MYTHS AND GHOSTS

The psychological games we learned as children, and played in order to survive, now threaten the survival of our adult relationships.

—The Paradox of Game-Playing

From the time we were very young, you and I developed behavior patterns and made early decisions in our lives to get the love we wanted. Aside from the usual child-like games we played, like jump rope, hide and seek and throw the ball, we formulated psychological games based on what was happening, what we thought was happening, and what we decided we needed to survive what was happening.

As we became adults, we unwittingly carried those psychological games with us into our friendships, our family relations, our love relationships — never realizing that we no longer needed them and that they would get in our way. So, we kept on playing and, as a result, struggling. It was always important for us to be right. It did not occur to us that in order to be right, we had to make somebody else wrong. We focused on the differences between us and wanted desperately to *fix* or *change* these people in our lives who simply did not know the right way to be.

Those innocent games we created to get us through our hard times, and the reactions we got from people we played the games with, gave us the sense of *right* and *wrong* we now hold that has fabricated our beliefs about people, love, marriage — everything. Some of these beliefs we hold close to our hearts. We give them value, credence, and we live our lives by them. I don't know how to break this to you gently: Many of those beliefs are lies. That's right; they are not true.

Now, I want to make sure you understand that you needed to believe these lies,
misconceptions, and myths like you needed your
games — in order to survive. There is no telling
the amount of anguish these games and misconceptions cause you now — yet, at one time, you
needed them. Now, as an adult, the time has
come for you to examine them and see them for
what they are. Many of them are causing the
struggles and problems prevalent in your relationships, and I want to help you work through them
so you can get on with the joy in your life.

There is a reason these games and
misconceptions don't go away: Their ghosts
continue to sit on our shoulders throughout our
adult lives — just like tiny mothers whispering,
"Don't forget to wash behind your ears." How
much are you reminded of your parents in some
of the things you say and do?

As children we were asked to con-
form to the wishes of our parents — to do and be
what they wanted. No one ever said, "Okay,
you're 40 years old — you don't have to wash
behind your ears if you don't want to." As a
result, every now and then, in the shower, that
voice is still there. And, as parents, we instruct our
own children to wash behind their ears — to do

and be what *we* want. And in *all* our relationships, we want others to do and be what we
want.

You can never love another person
enough to condone changing yourself in order to
meet that person's preferences and expectations. In the same way, you cannot expect another person to show his or her love by changing
for you. Yet, that's what we want and we continue to ask for it. Some of the things you learned
to do in your childhood you continue to do now.
The reason? This behavior is the only behavior
you learned to get you through that situation.

The Games We Play

Some of those psychological games
we've played, since childhood, lead to the decisions we make in our lives today. Here are some
examples:

Any Attention Is Better Than None.
Your father may pay no attention to
you, except when you spill milk; then
your father slaps you. From this you
learn how to get attention and,
believing that this painful attention is
better than none, you keep doing

things to get it. The guys at the federal prison play this game.

Sit On Daddy's Lap.
As a little girl, you discover that when you sit on your father's lap and ask for something you want, you get it. At age 28, you ask your husband for a new car. When he says you cannot afford it, you sit on his lap and plead. When he still insists you cannot afford it, you get angry and feel rejected. That game you learned as a child doesn't work for you now, yet you continue to use it. It's the only game you know.

Let's Not Communicate.
If your partner asks you, "What time is it?" and you answer, "It's 10:45" — communication is complete. Someone asked a question; someone answered it. If, however, your partner asks, "What time is it?" and you respond, "Don't you ever wear a watch?" there is no communication. There is a fight. You begin with the time of day and you wind up arguing about responsibility, politics, in-laws

or the kids, because when you re-
sponded to your partner's question,
you had something else on your
mind.

Whatever caused you to respond
with anything other than the correct time has to
do with games you've learned and myths you
believe. Perhaps you once had a boss who used
to interrupt your work every five minutes to ask
the time. Maybe you believe that if someone
asks you the time, this puts you in an inferior position; and because your partner asked you the
time, you feel he may think he is superior to you.

There are innumerable reasons you
might have for snapping at your partner, none of
which have anything to do with your partner.
The point is that there was no communication.
The question was never answered. Can you think
of times in your life when there was no communication when you asked a question? Can you
think of times in your life when you never answered a question? I can, on both counts.

My wife: "Did you get the clothes
from the cleaners?"
Me: "How was I supposed to remember to do that?"

Me: "Did you close the garage door?"
My wife: "Why do you want it closed?"

As years go by, manipulations escalate to deep resentments when couples haven't cleared the air of their hurt feelings. These resentments are the basis for more games. We never satisfy the *kid* in us who didn't get what he or she wanted, and we continue to play out the circumstances of these games in our adult relationships. We played these games in order to survive; now that we are adults, sometimes we continue to play these games even though they don't work anymore — even though we don't *need* them anymore.

Although we are now adults, voices of our parents, grandparents, teachers and guardians still echo in our heads. Their ghosts sit on our shoulders and still tell us what we "should" do and how we will suffer if we don't. We must get a hold of these ghosts — see them for what they are — and kick them out the door, once and for all.

Crossed communications go on in love relationships all the time. They can build into deep resentments if the air is not cleared. These resentments, which are blown up because of game playing and belief in certain myths, become the basis for more game-playing, more myth building; and, in a matter of time, couples have grown so far apart that their once not-so-different differences have become as distant as the sun and the moon.

The irony is that most of us want the same things in our lives. We're looking for comfort in relationships, companionship, sharing, giving and fulfillment of our needs. We play child-like games and believe they will get us what we want and what we need. We don't see that playing these games actually brings us the exact opposite.

Furthermore, what we've been taught about game-playing of any kind is that somebody wins and somebody loses. In most sports competitions, there is a winner and a loser. Life doesn't have to be that way. I hear you. You're saying, that's impossible — both sides cannot win. And I say it's a misconception that we cannot both win. Society has taught us to *believe* that only one side can win, and this simply is not true. I promise, I will show you how.

The Myths We Believe

A myth, as traditionally defined, is a story that explains a practice or belief. No one ever knows where these stories come from, yet everyone knows one or two. My favorite, about a newly married couple, goes like this:

The Ham Ends

A young bride cuts the ends off a ham she is preparing for a Sunday dinner. Asked by her husband why she cut the ends off, she explains that is how a ham is cooked. Not satisfied, he asks his mother-in-law about this method of preparation. She says her mother was a fine cook and always took the ends off a ham before cooking. Still not satisfied, at a family gathering the young groom asks the grandmother why she cuts the ends off a ham. The grand-mother answers, "Because my pan isn't big enough to hold a whole ham."

"Myths?" you say, appalled by the very idea. "I don't have any myths in my life; I'm very realistic."

Some of your myths and misconceptions may be so well hidden that you are not even aware they are there; once more, the existence of one usually leads to the existence of many more, so I would bet you live with several. Tell me honestly that you have not believed one of these at one time or another:

One person is to blame for a breakup.

A problem can be reconciled without talking about it.

If love is real, it will last forever.

Most of the time, we have no idea of the origin of the myths we hold, including myths about our marriage. But they are there, sure as the air we breathe. There are good reasons why you have carried these with you all your life. However, the time has come for you to see them for what they are and let them go.

It's painful to talk about those things that hurt. Some subjects are so painful to us that we have successfully covered over our feelings about them and are no longer in touch with them. Society has helped us tranquilize these feelings and taught us that we can always take a pill, smoke a cigarette, eat sugar, aerobicize, go shopping.

We've come to expect rapid explanations, immediate answers, instantaneous resolutions. Thus, we have come to believe in one of the most lethal misconceptions of all:

#1 **There is a cure-all, quick fix for my marriage.**

> Larry, a busy litigation attorney, brought Jeanine into therapy because she was giving him a hard time about his long work hours. He gave her money for anything she wanted; he made certain that she was sexually accommodated as often as she liked; and still, he complained, she was not happy. He wanted to know if I could *fix* her. In his eyes, she was the problem, and she was the one who needed therapy. Larry believed that money and sexual gratification were the solutions to Jeanine's pain.

There was a more serious disease to be treated in their relationship. The real causes of Jeanine's hurt and anger were far more deep-seated and reflective of attitudes and expectations she had been carrying around for years. She and her mother had been similarly neglected by her workaholic father, and what Jeanine needed more than anything from Larry was his time and attention, two commodities that he could not quickly dispense and forget.

Society gives us immediate gratification — fast food, fast cars. A car salesman will make sure you drive a new car off the lot today, because he knows that if you wait until tomorrow, you might not buy the car. With personal problems, however, gratification is rarely immediate.

In this new age, we are stuck with an old-fashioned paradox: Solutions come more quickly when you accept the fact that there is *no quick fix*.

There are two reasons for this:

1.   **Smokescreens.** People tend to focus on peripheral issues and smokescreens before getting to the real intensity of their hurt. We humans

need time to find our way through the forest of our defenses.

2. **Solutions are rarely immediate.** When bones are broken, they must knit. When seeds are planted, they must germinate and grow. When relationships are in trouble, they need the benefit of communication and reconciliation. All these processes take time.

Let's take a look at some sample issues. Perhaps you have been focusing on a smokescreen issue and simply didn't know. You might want to make a list of your own issues and see how they compare to these. First the smokescreen, then the real issue:

Smokescreen vs. *Belief*

There's not enough money.
I believe our house should look better than our neighbors' house.

There's not enough sex.
I expect that there will be sex often: three times a week.

He never helps around the house on weekends. He's off playing golf.

> *I believe we should be together on weekends.*

She's always on the phone with her boss.

> *Women are not trustworthy. I don't trust her out working.*

Dinner is never waiting when I come home.

> *She ought to be home taking care of the family.*

I don't enjoy parties that involve lots of people.

> *People might ask me what I do for a living, and I'm not proud of what I do.*

Where did your belief come from? Did you learn it from your father? Your mother? Your grandparents? A special friend?

You may believe everything will get fixed if there's more money. The real issue, however, may be that you believe a big and beautiful home is the measure of your worth. This belief could be something that was instilled in you in early childhood. Not having enough money, therefore, is only a symptom — not the disease itself. In the same way, believing there's not enough sex between you and your partner can be a symptom of a belief you have.

The real causes of our differences are expectations, attitudes and beliefs. Sorting these out takes time and talk; it takes getting into the essence of who we are. In this *quick fix* society in which we live, many of us are not willing to spend the time or give the attention required to do this. My feeling is that if you care about what happens to the relationship, you simply must.

#2 If my partner understood me, he'd change.

Jacqueline wanted Steve to see her point of view — that she was doing everything in her power to be the woman that he wanted her to be. She said, "If he would just understand that I've become everything he has expected of me, he would see that I'm perfect for him and he would love me."

Stop working on getting your partner to *see* your problem. We think that if our partners *understand* our problems, they will change or agree with us. Not so. If your partner sees or understands that you need something from him, he may make a change to please you. This is not necessarily a change he truly wants to make. Such a change will be short-lived. Focus must not be on understanding problems. Focus must be on solutions.

The Problem
    The Solution

My partner doesn't *see* that I need some time to myself.
    Make time for yourself.

I would like to get my partner to *see* who I am.
    Be who you are.

My partner doesn't work hard enough to make the money we need for what I want.
    Become a high wage earner yourself.

My partner isn't *aware* that I need the garage door to be shut.
    Close the garage door.

    #3 If you really loved me, you would know what I want.

    Laura wanted Gary to know her so

well that he would be able to fulfill her every need without her having to ask him for anything. When he didn't automatically pick up that she wanted to eat out that night, or watch something special on TV, or needed a hug, she became angry.

Insisting that others be mind readers, and never exposing our wants, allows us to blame someone else and to shoulder no responsibility for what we want in our lives. I can hear you now. You're saying, after all this time, there are certain things she should know about you. There are certain ways he should remember to please you. No, I'm sorry. I am certain there are times when your partner does remember and does please you and does exactly what you want. You should be happy for those. Those are wonderful moments. All those other times when you want something and your partner simply is not aware, you must ask. The more you ask, the more often your partner will be made aware of your desires and the more able he or she will become familiar with what you want.

Please remember that *asking* for what you want and *demanding* what you want are two different things.

#4 You should always be interested in what I have to say.

Herman and Mildred, after many years of marriage, were now in their 60s and retired. They were having trouble chatting because they no longer had business details to dis- cuss. Each felt neglected by the other. Mildred said Herman didn't really listen to her properly. Herman felt Mildred had lost interest in him because he no longer came home with "war" stories.

In their discussions, instead of asking, "Why aren't you listening to me?" I suggested they ask each other, "What are you thinking about?" Mildred learned that Horace was fanta- sizing about a long trip to the Northwest. She loved to travel. That became something they talked about incessantly and dreamed about together.

It's a fact of life: you and your part- ner are not always going to be 100% interested in what each other has to say. When, however, you take an interest in your partner's thoughts and feelings, ask about them, and honestly talk about them — there's a good chance your interest level is going to go up. We are all fascinating creatures, once we get to know one another for who we truly are.

#5 We will always be the same as we are now.

Sandy wanted to get a job after her youngest child began to go to school full time. John objected to Sandy's employment. He complained bitterly about dinner not being served "on time." That, however, was his smokescreen issue. Actually, John's objection was based on his fear that Sandy would make more money than he. John enjoyed the role of No. 1 bread winner. He felt threatened by Sandy's employment, and these feelings overcame his recognition that Sandy's job would contribute more income to the family budget and, best of all, make Sandy feel good about herself.

This misconception can be the basis for so many misunderstandings. Because our struggle to get what we want is sometimes based on a fear of change, we will sometimes do anything to *not* change. Perhaps it is human nature to wallow in the comfort of staying the same rather than risking discomfort to find out who we really are. We all do it. We live roles instead of our selves.

To have the expectation that we will always be the same as we are now is to say that we will never grow and never be open to accepting new possibilities for ourselves as they emerge. Is that something you want to say? I don't.

#6 Sex should be wonderful all the time, like it appears in the movies.

Sam was terrified to be genuinely affectionate toward Maureen. His message to her was "Don't get too close." He rejected her hugs and attempts at closeness unless he was in the mood for sex. Therapy brought up the severe rejection and sexual abuse he suffered as a child. When Maureen saw that Sam's early conditioning was the source of his distance and not her, she was able

to stop demanding contact and
accept what he was able to offer
her, even when it was simply a smile
or a wave.

As their therapy progressed, Sam
was able to say to her, "I'm scared when I get
close to you." Through Maureen's acceptance
of that, his fear lessened and eventually he was
able to sit with his arm around her and hold her.

I heard a man once say that every
sex act he had performed was "right on the
money." He was talking about orgasms. Sex is
more than orgasms. Priorities change for all of us.
When we first meet, a brandy in front of the fire-
place on a bearskin rug in black tie and velvet
can be very exciting. There comes a time, however, when the comfortableness of looking
across the room and smiling an intimate, knowing
smile to one another may be all we need.

In believing sex should be wonderful
all the time, your focus is on the act of sex, rather
than on the act of loving, sharing, trusting and
committing. Where there is love, sex *is* absolutely
wonderful — most of the time — unless, of course,
your partner has forgotten to close the garage
door, or something important like that.

#7 Every relationship should be absolutely 50/50.

It is impossible for two people to measure their contributions equally. The act of such an analysis is the antithesis of love, because it demonstrates no interest in the satisfaction or security of the other person. Sometimes my wife and I are 60/40; sometimes 25/75; sometimes 90/10 and 5/95. It depends on what is going on in our lives at the time and who needs what, when. Loving behavior is being less concerned with who is giving how much, and being more concerned with what is in the best interest of the union at this time.

#8 I can get everything I need from one person.

Early in marriage, being the special one, the only one, is very important. But if you do not grow beyond this belief, you may wind up in trouble. You will come to expect too much from one another. It is impossible to depend on one person to give you everything you want in life. Each of us secretly wants to be that very special one for someone else, like we wanted to be for Mom; yet who of us can point to one person who can be the be-all, end-all for us. It is important to have other people in our lives to spend time with, and having these other people usually makes us more appreciative of one another when we get back home.

#9 Women are responsible for the relationship.

You've heard this before: Men are responsible for making the money; women are responsible for the relationship. While we certainly have let go of the belief that a woman's place is only in the home, the concept that women are responsible for the relationship has not been relinquished as readily. Even modern women's magazines reflect this cultural myth, offering women a plethora of ways to make their men happy.

What utterly amazes me is that women believe this myth as much as men do. They come to therapy asking what they can do to save the marriage; they come wondering where they went wrong and how they are deficient. "This isn't important to him. It is to me, so I'm here." Their belief is that they alone are responsible for making everything work.

#10 A knight in shining armor will save me.

Romance novels, the best-selling fiction in the country, always depict a woman, sometimes a strong woman, who is finally rescued in the end by a man. Women who read these novels want, more than anything, to be saved by a knight in shining armor and will do anything to get this.

How did women wind up believing in the contradiction that they must be rescued by a man, and yet they are responsible for the relationship?

#11 I have to take care of others' needs before my own.

Living for everyone except yourself is bargain basement living. It is a deprived lifestyle. You are so busy being concerned with those around you, you neglect your own essence, your own spirituality, your own being. When you hear yourself say, "For Mom and Dad I need to be...," "For my partner I need to be..." — be on guard. This is not having it all; this is spreading yourself thin. True having-it-all is having intimacy and contact with your self, owning your own sense of individuality so that when you come into contact with family and friends you have something to give them.

#12 Trying is the same as doing.

Would you take a plane trip if you thought the pilot was going to *try* to get from New York to Los Angeles? Maybe Orville and Wilbur Wright were willing to take that chance. I'm not. Likewise, if you and I have a problem in our relationship, and I tell you I am going to *try* to be more sensitive to your needs, are you going to feel satisified with that? If you need me to be sensitive to your needs, you must tell me: I need this. Do it, or don't do it. Whatever my decision is in response will determine whether or not you are going to make a change in your life.

The truth about *trying* is that you are saying you are doing something and you really are not. If you say you are trying, you are, for the most part, doing just the opposite. Trying is, in a sense, rebelling, holding back, saying "I'm not going to give 100%." It is our way of rebelling against what we feel is power over us. Rebelling changes nothing and benefits no one.

#13 Confrontation is harmful to a relationship.

Those of us who believe that confrontation harms our relationships are simply
afraid of it. Somewhere in our past we have
experienced unpleasant, perhaps terrifying confrontations. Actually, honest confrontation is in
the best interest of a relationship. It need not be
violent and need not disregard the needs of
either partner. Confrontation can be a positive,
forward-moving energy that forces partners to
deal with each other, talk to each other, get to
know each other. Only through confrontation
can partners discover whether or not they are
able to work things out.

In Paul and Mary's marriage, Mary
was expected to do whatever Paul
didn't want to do. He was a master
at being passive or aggressive,
whichever suited his purposes. When
Mary confronted Paul and in essence asked him if he wanted a
partner or an employee, she discov-
ered that he wanted an employee.
So she left. Had Paul been interested in a real partner, they might
have worked things out. But since
he was not, if she had never con-

fronted Paul, she might still be
caught up in his game.

You can spend years — perhaps a
lifetime — believing something that is not true,
believing your partner loves you, believing your
partner will change — believing simply because
you cannot bear the thought of *not* believing.

#14 A problem can be reconciled without talking about it.

We live in hope that a problem will
resolve itself. It rarely does, and anything uncom-
fortable that goes undiscussed winds up growing;
before long, there's a 19-foot purple elephant
sitting in the middle of your house — everyone
knows it's there and no one will talk about it. You
will hear yourselves talking about bedroom wall-
paper or how the TV reception isn't clear, in one
moment, and then you will find yourselves swear-
ing at each other in the next. Take note: This is
your cue that it's time to clear the smokescreen
and confront the real issue.

We are scared to let our partners
know all there is to know about us, because we
think that knowing may spoil their fantasies —
and ours. Part of the fear is, "If you really know

me, you won't like me." And, "If you know all about me, you'll use what you know against me." The truth is just the opposite. When couples *don't* face their real hurt, their regard for one another diminishes.

Face up to your real hurt, or your regard for one another will be lost. If you lose mutual regard, you will become more concerned with the *image* of your marriage — the illusion of what *good* people are supposed to do and how they're supposed to do it — than with who you truly are and why you feel the way you do. Don't let this happen. It's too important.

In many cases, someone will say, "Now I feel as if I know you, and I really love you." More astounding is when someone says, as they will, once intimacy has been achieved, "Now I feel I know you, and I love you *more* than I did before." If you are looking for reconciliation, start listening and start talking. You won't be sorry.

#15 I should never expose my true feelings so much that I am vulnerable.

It can be frightening to be vulnerable. Most likely you have had people in your life, as I have had in mine, who have taken ad-

vantage of your vulnerability and failed to support you when you needed strength. When we
do take the risk, and tell the truth about how we
feel in a given situation, that feeling of telling the
truth and honestly expressing how we feel gives
us more strength than we could possibly have by
withholding that truth. When we do *not* say what
is in our hearts, we lose power. The more we
expose our true feelings, the less vulnerable we
are. Honesty is very powerful.

#16 A secret agenda is sometimes necessary and less hazardous than telling the truth.

Secret agendas are what we create
to get what we want when be believe that our
partner is opposed to what we want. The reason
we keep this agenda a secret is that we fear it
will be used against us. Those of us who repress
our feelings often have secret agendas. We
make them secret because we have been led to
believe that what we really want is contrary to
what we *should* want. We are fearful of disap-
proval.

Mary Elizabeth always wanted to be
a nun. Bowing to family pressure,
she got married and had seven

children. Now her children are grown and she spends all her time working for the altar society. Her husband has now made enough money to relax, travel and do things they've always talked about doing. She won't leave town because she is always *needed* at the altar society meetings. He is confused and cannot figure out why she will not let go of those meetings.

Mary Elizabeth doesn't want her secret agenda to be found out. She continually covers over her feelings rather than reveal them. She lives her life being careful, accommodating and diplomatic rather than being truthful. Every time Mary Elizabeth uses her secret agenda, her husband feels disappointed and she doesn't feel good about herself. But she keeps on using this agenda, because it's all she knows how to do.

When there isn't the intimacy to share your real agenda, communication breaks down. If you have trouble taking people at their face value, if you add extra meanings to what is being said and second-guess people in your life, cautiously hedging your bets — there's a good chance you have a secret agenda that needs airing. Stop wasting your precious energy. Life is too short to live a lie.

#17 **We need bargaining chips to make a relationship work.**

I have used bargaining chips in my life whenever I felt I had to do something I didn't want to do. The typical bargaining chip sentence goes like this:

Okay, *I* won't yell at the kids, if *you*...

All right, *I* won't spend money, if *you*...

Here's the deal: *I* won't have an affair, if *you*...

At those times when we feel out of control and unable to get what we want, there is a tendency to use these "I won't...if you won't" retorts. Bargaining chips may produce change. This kind of change, however, will be short-lived. The reason? These promises are dishonest, hurtful, and do not resolve the problem and are, therefore, impossible to maintain.

The acceptance of tradeoffs and deals is a stalemate, a cold war. Rather than use power to manipulate, find the power and strength to be truthful. What you want is to evaluate, rather than make a deal. Evaluations are based on caring. Tradeoffs and deals take on a flavor of litigation, and you can almost sense the attorney hovering in the background.

Instead of saying, "I'll do what you want if you do what I want," say: "I've got to survive and you're taking all I've got in me with these tradeoffs; you're wearing me down. I can't or won't do that anymore." This is making a decision. This is a reconciliation.

Rather than creating a distance between you with a bargaining chip statement like, "I won't spend money, if you won't spend money," ask questions like:

> "What's in the best interest of the budget today?"

> "Can *we* work this out so *we* can get that?"

> "What can *we* do to make us *both* happy?"

Re-evaluating your relationship — especially when there are changes — a new child, a new job, a major illness — can be just what the doctor ordered. Sometimes taking stock every two or three years, for no particular reason, is refreshing, loving, productive. Companies use this process all the time to make sure that they are moving forward and that their employees are happy. Why not life partners?

#18 A spouse will *always* forgive a spouse of infidelity.

Hank and Elaine have been married for 25 years; she had been a quiet, closet alcoholic for the last 15. When she made a change about a year ago, and decided to live her life sober, she started standing up for herself. Hank was stunned and immediately had an affair with another woman.

Hank and Elaine are now discussing putting their marriage back together, and Hank insists that his affair was "one little indiscretion" that does not matter. To Elaine, it does matter. Although she now understands why he did it, she still feels she has no basis for trusting Hank. It is common for men to believe that their wives will overlook and forgive an affair. Elaine, however, knows she has alternatives, and if she can find no basis for trusting Hank, she will opt for divorce.

#19 A spouse will *never* forgive a spouse of infidelity.

Nathan chipped away at Opal's self-respect almost from their wedding night — constantly telling her to be grateful to him because if he had not married her, no one else ever would have. Opal reached the point where she needed to test her attractiveness and, in desperation, she had an affair. When Nathan found out, he was devastated. Before long, however, he began to feel he needed and wanted Opal. The affair made her more attractive to him. He forgave her the infidelity and they are working on renewing their relationship. The irony is that Opal now has a sense of her self worth and is questioning whether Nathan contributes to it.

Infidelity on the part of either partner, or both, can be forgiven when both parties are able to make a full recommitment to their relationship. This takes a confrontation of myths as well as examination of beliefs and behaviors that led to the infidelity in the first place. I know, you are saying, this will take months of therapy. The truth is that it could. But if both partners are strongly interested in recommitment, all work can be done at home, without a therapist. Once you make the *commitment* to confront and evaluate, you are on your way.

#20 I am obligated to reconcile for my parents.

When Marian got out of a bad marriage, she was afraid to tell her parents. She remembered her father saying many years before, "If we ever have a divorce in this family, I'll have a heart attack." She was terrified that they would never speak to her again, so she wrote a letter instead of calling them. In a letter she received from her parents, they wrote: "Dear Marian: We understand your predicament; it's unfortunate, but these things happen in life. Your dad and I are going to play bridge tomorrow night..." Marian was angry. "They don't care," she said. "I lived my life their way so long, and they don't care."

Marian had been using her family all her life as an excuse not to do those things she was scared to do. She didn't realize this until we talked about the letter she received from them.

If you feel in your heart that you must get back together with your partner to please your family, you must ask yourself if your family is an excuse to reconcile your relationship, and you must ask yourself what would happen if you did not please your family. Would they survive if you did what you needed to do for yourself?

If you didn't get permission and protection to express yourself when you were a child, you're not going to get that from your parents now. The terror of breaking out of the family system is fear of losing acceptance, a sense of losing your roots. It's important to reach the point where you think and say, "I'm not living my life for you." Any other reaction is choosing to stay within the family system. It's deciding to stay, because there must be some kind of payoff. It may not be a payoff you need or want; rather, a payoff you're used to.

In claiming your own potential, the resolution is to quit hooking into other people's expectations. Your antenna has to be up; you have to be aware of when you're getting hooked. Don't fall into the trap of doing what you're "supposed to do." Whatever you do, take action because you want to, need to, love to.

#21 I am obligated to reconcile for my children.

This is a hard one, I know. Reconciliation cannot, however, be done for others — not even for the children, because, in the long run, it is very unhealthy for children to live in homes where their parents are constantly angry, threatening and abusive.

When couples get caught up in who is *right*, underneath their apparent interest in working things out, there is sometimes the desire to hang in until a spouse is proven *wrong*. They get caught up in proving this to everybody, including the children. If you truly love your children, you can give to them as an individual just as much as you can as a married person. Sometimes more.

Divorce can be in the best interest of the children, particularly when the alternative is exposing them to incest, abuse, drugs and alcohol; divorce is better than using them as pawns in toxic games played by people in pain.

The most important things the children need to know are:

Their parents love them, even though they may not love each other.

They are not to blame for the separation of their parents.

Separation is better for everyone, although difficult to get through right now.

#22 Couples can always work out staying together.

Ellen realized, after living 10 years with Steve, that he would never change from being a lazy, double-dealing person. Worse, she had spent 10 years supporting him, helping him be the person he was. When, in therapy, she saw that nothing she could do would make any difference, she was crushed. She had to own up to the fact that Steve would always be the way he was. She had been invested, all these years, in getting him to change.

Sometimes *working it out* means staying together; sometimes it means separation. Sometimes the best solution involves working with a counselor, a third party — someone who says, "Look at the absurdity of this. Are you guys going to keep doing this to one another, or what?"

#23 If I change to please him, he will never leave.

Phyllis, who was once attractive to Donald because she was so special, so distinct, had to deal with the fact that Donald wanted her to change — to become more like him. She didn't want to change. She also didn't want to lose him. So she changed. To her dismay, he left anyway.

When Phyllis became what Donald said he wanted, he lost interest in her. The challenge was over. Donald was one of those people who needs to make demands, who needs to be *right* by making his partner wrong. Changing to hold on to your partner will never, ever work. Don't do it.

#24 Our relationship will be easy after reconciliation.

Paula and David are a young married couple who work together. Paula is an open, friendly, chatty young woman, a real asset in working with customers. David saw her as being flirty and seductive and was terrified of her leaving him. The only way for Paula to alleviate David's fears was to not be herself and to cut off her aliveness and joy of living.

When they sought help in therapy, David thought Paula would always be the friendly, open woman he fell in love with. The kind of woman she is is what drew him to her in the first place. He began to see that she was not at fault and that he really would not want her to change.

Rather than blaming Paula or attempting to manipulate her, David took the 180°

turn and started to deal with his own fears. This was their turning point. This reconciliation has certainly clarified their relationship; however, David and Paula both see that their new knowledge is not a quick fix and that there is a great deal of work they must do with each other to ensure that their new awareness remains clear and well-defined. The problem could re-surface; and if it does, they must deal with it again and again. What matters, however, is that they care enough about one another to keep working. As long as that is there, they will be able to work things out.

Ghosts That Haunt Us

The ghosts of the past are in all of us. Our conflicts are rooted in our early decisions, family myths, and how we hear and deal with expectations. The ghosts we all have are the you-betters, you've-got-tos, and you-shoulds that we bring from our childhood to our adult relationships. Mom and Dad, Uncle George, Aunt Emma, Father John and our first-grade teacher are alive and well in our houses. They raise their heads whenever a situation reminds us of situations in the past, and they demand that we respond in our old way of responding within that family system.

If your partner has an emotional scene, and you cannot understand how such a small situation could cause such a scene, rest assured that the ghosts of the past have popped up. The healing process is to talk, to look at the ghosts and to make new decisions — such as, "We will not allow these ghosts in our kitchen, our bedroom, or anywhere else in the house. As long as they are around, we cannot see one another or ourselves."

We often don't see a situation in a relationship for what it is. Instead, we see the myth. The wedding night, how to raise children, how to maintain a house, appropriate standards of living — all these situations have huge systems of myth and misconception wrapped around them.

Growth involves stretching our self-imposed boundaries to include parts of ourselves that we previously rejected or have never even recognized. When we run away from any frustration that might be painful and look for shortcuts, the result is lack of growth.

Sometimes a lot of disappointment comes when we begin to see through our myths. We start to understand that they are a hoax, that we contributed to them, and sometimes based our lives on them. As disappointing as this can be, once we deal with these myths — share them, dispel them and, hopefully, reach a point where we can laugh at them — an enormous amount of energy is released, energy we can use in our real life.

George, The Tour Guide

George was a fat, lonely man who had difficulty maintaining employment. He believed the myth that he had to lose weight before he could seek employment. He had been to Overeaters Anonymous, Weight Watchers and other organizations. I told him that the weight problem was a smokescreen, and that his fear of employment was real. I told him that somehow he was going to have to "get on the bus," and get going and doing. George terminated therapy, holding on to his myth.

Four months later, I received a photograph of him, wearing a uniform, standing next to a tour bus. On the back he had written, "I got on the bus."

4

LOVE

Loving someone is letting them go.

—The Paradox of Love

What Is Love?

In the beginning, we make a lot of
our own magic in a new relationship. We fall in
love with one another's "differences" — the
things that are unique about us. We are excited

by the surprises, the chemistry, the hopes about each other. We go on picnics, take walks, buy ice cream cones, hold hands — all of these are fun. We fantasize that this will last forever, this is how we are, this will always be.

Then the magic starts to slip. Sex starts to lose its mystique; the things we associate with love begin to lose their significance. There are no more great romantic scenes, fewer flowers, the negligees get worn less and less, and sex becomes functional — more out of need than out of love, romance, fun and playfulness. Our beliefs about life, our assumptions about roles, and our needs left over from childhood and other relationships come between us and intrude on our hopes and dreams.

Here's what happens. As much as we enjoy being with people who are just like us, who think like us and share similar likes and dislikes, when we fall in love, we are strongly attracted to someone who is different from us. "Why?" you ask. There are lots of theories. Many say we are naturally attracted to someone who acts as a "complement" to us — someone who is a balance for us and winds up teaching us what we need to learn in life.

For whatever reason, what happens is that an early bird, for example, becomes attracted to a night owl. An attorney who spends most of his day behind a desk is attracted to a stewardess who spends her life flying all over the world. When the morning person moves in with the night owl, when the attorney marries the stewardess, problems arise. The morning person and the night owl notice a lag in their sexual relationship because they sleep at different times. The attorney complains that the stewardess is never around; the stewardess complains that the attorney can never get away. The very differences that attracted these partners to one another now upset them.

How do they deal with these differences? How do they figure out what is important in order to give both a sense of well-being? For isn't that what happiness is — having a sense of well-being?

Because these two people see differences where exciting opposites used to be, they focus on those differences and they struggle, both within themselves and with whomever they have these differences. What they fail to recognize is that by engaging in these struggles, they paradoxically wind up creating for themselves the exact opposite of what they truly want.

I know. You're saying, "Why would I intentionally go after the exact opposite of what I want?" I don't think you do this intentionally, yet I'm willing to bet that you do it. When all you want from your partner is that he love you, why would you treat him as if he purposely put your favorite cotton sweater in the hot washload and shrank it to a size 1? If that woman in your life is so important to you, why would you treat her as if she cheated on you just because an old lover called her up to say hello? You want love from this person, and you just screamed at this person. And when you screamed, you got the exact opposite of love, right? See?

"Love" is the most abused word in the English language. It can lead us to exhilarating fun; and it can be used as a weapon, to manipulate and instill guilt. The problem begins when we fall in love with the image of love rather than make contact with what I believe love really is — the spiritual essence in people.

According to Harry Stack Sullivan, a psychiatrist, love exists when the satisfaction or security of another person becomes as important to us as our own satisfaction or security. Instead of saying, "If you stop drinking, flirting, working late, ignoring me — then we'll have a happy marriage," love is saying,   "I love you for who you are and who you are not. I accept that you drink, flirt, work late, ignore me. However, to take care of myself, I need to go to Al-Anon, I need to find a job, I need to join a therapy group." Or, love is saying, "I can no longer accept that you drink, flirt, work late, ignore me. It hurts me to see you hurt yourself. Yes, I love you, and yes, I'm going to have to leave."

If you say to me, "You're acting like a jerk — cut it out!" perhaps I had it coming. I'm glad you said this instead of resenting me all day. If you had kept this feeling to yourself, we would have had a terrible day. You would have shown your resentment in other ways, and I'd never know what was upsetting you. Therefore, by taking care of yourself, you took care of me and put an end to the whole game. The confusion we feel between our role (perfect husband/ perfect wife) and our essence (who we are) is the cornerstone of all our games, the source of all our problems in relationships.

**When partners are not who they
really are, a marriage can continue.
The relationship, however, is gone.**

Isn't it amusing that we spend our
childhood growing up, learning to be *the perfect
child*, who will grow into *the perfect man, the
perfect woman, the perfect husband, the perfect wife, the perfect father, mother, employer,
employee....* the list goes on and on? Then we
spend our entire adult life *un*learning the confusing roles we learned to play.

You cannot go on pretending that
love is enough. It is no longer acceptable to say,
"I love you, so let me go on being the selfish,
uncaring person I am." Or, "I love you, so I'll just
live with your drinking." Or, "I love you, what else
matters?" We pretend love is enough; we want it
to excuse our behavior. You must love your self
enough to set limits on your behavior in a relationship. If these limits are not accepted and
agreed to between partners, the problems are
going to mount.

Love is:

Getting to know your essence.

Respecting yourself.

Being who you are.

Saying what you feel.

Getting to know your partner's essence.

Knowing when love is not enough.

Love And The Media

In today's world we face external, fast-moving changes in our culture. We read books, watch movies, television. We get a lot of messages about what love ought to be. Many of these are Utopian ideals, misconceptions or myths.

We've already mentioned romance novels. Talk about unreal expectations! Millions of women are subconsciously led to believe that a woman, no matter how strong, is, in the end, always rescued by a knight in shining armor. Any man who reads these novels is led to believe he's supposed to *be* a knight in shining armor. Millions of people watch television soap operas and believe that their lives ought to be like those they see acted out. We don't stop to realize that these actors go home to their real life situations and face the same problems we do.

Advertising is no help. The propaganda we get from commercials we see on television, or magazine ads we browse through is dangerous. TV ads tell us if we use this toothpaste, wear this perfume, put on this aftershave, we will have love. If I make this kind of coffee, he'll never leave me. If I buy this kind of car, she's going to love me.

While we look at those advertisements and know in our hearts that there's an advertiser selling us a product, we are still influenced by these images and subsconsciously we are buying what that product has to sell: Sex, love, acceptance, whatever is missing in our lives. Add these hard and soft sells to the inner conflicts we already have, and we become victims of a double-edged sword.

Love Is Finding Ways To Agree

Life for most people is a struggle of relating. In my 25 years as a counselor and therapist, I've noticed that most people sabotage their relationships by insisting: "If you love me, you'll always want what I want — you'll support me, even when I'm wrong; listen to me, no matter how you're feeling; have sex with me even if you don't want it." That's not love talking.

Love says, "Yes, I love you, and I still want to take this job even if dinner is not on the table by 6:00 p.m." Love is saying, "Yes, I love you, and no, I cannot support you on this decision." Love is saying, "What do we do together to work this out?"

If I don't understand you, and you don't understand me, love is agreeing that we don't understand each other. Based on this agreement, we can find other areas in which we agree. The more we find areas of agreement, the more we are able to love one another, as well as accept, trust and feel good about our selves and each other. When we are not okay with our selves, we make the other person feel as bad as we feel. Love is then used to manipulate or blame.

We stop having a good relationship when one or both of us stop feeling good about who we are.

There is no one way to love or make love. Some of us grow up believing that the way we love is the only way; some grow up believing that the way we love is *wrong*. Love is what you feel for another person, and the way you express it is yours. Your partner's way is his or hers.

Accepting one another's differences here is essential. In order to understand what love means to one another, we must show it, talk about it, share it.

No one person can love us enough to fill all of our needs. Love, therefore, also means letting go. It means you and your partner love one another all you are possibly capable of loving one another. Then you must let your partner go and share portions of his or her life with other people. Love between your partner and yourself is understanding the different loves you have for different people, knowing that the love between the two of you is unique — it's romantic, life supporting — the kind of love that has caused you to decide to live your lives together.

Love is asking: 'What are you thinking about?" instead of "Why aren't you listening to me?" It's asking questions and creating mutual learning about one another. Most of us want the same things — understanding, trust, esteem; however, we want them differently. When we talk about, accept, even celebrate our differences, we can develop a healthy way of supporting each other and our relationship.

We all have a window through which we see the world. When two people decide to share their lives, they have a choice to make about how they will look through their windows. Instead of continuing to look through both windows, many couples wind up looking through only one — and throw the other away. This may be done in the name of love, yet, in reality, it is not love. Love is keeping both windows open — sometimes looking through one, sometimes the other — most often, both.

Sex, Tenderness and Affection

My grandmother used to say, "If there are rocks in the bed, there are rocks in the marriage." Sex is important in our lives. It's one of the major breakdowns in marriages. We have great expectations of sex. Sexual differences and preferences can be grave differences in marriage. There are lots of variations, some of which turn people into things-to-have instead of people-to-be-with.

Making love happens when there is trust. When there is no trust, we don't make love, we just perform sexually. Making love with trust is satisfying. There are no doubts; we don't need variations to feel satisfied.

Tenderness is an important part of love. Many people associate tenderness only with sex. It is nonetheless an expression we can associate with all our behavior. Natural tenderness exists in all of us. It's the greatest essential quality to experiencing life in a joyful way. If rejected, however, tenderness may not be offered again. Tenderness can be the most complex, simple, frightening expression there is, because we feel vulnerable when we express it.

Babies express tenderness naturally. They don't care if you're tall, short, skinny, fat, ugly or good looking.

Somewhere between infancy and adulthood, tenderness disappears from a lot of people, to the point where very few will set themselves up for it anymore. I see pacifying, or placating, yet rarely the real, essential child-like, joyful tenderness — like when babies put their hands on your face. Without tenderness for your partner, there's nothing left except pretense.

A hug, recognition, or a touch when you walk by — could save a lot of marriages. It's like saying, "I'm here. I love you. We're okay."

5

DIFFERENCES

Accepting differences
between us produces
connections; efforts to
change differences
divides us.

—The Paradox of Differences

"We had to divorce. There was no
other way. We're so different,"
William says sadly.

"The secret of our marriage is the
fact that we're so different," Carol

says with a smile, as she holds hands
with Jim, her husband of 30 years.

When I was a kid, as soon as some-
one or something was labeled *different*, I was
instantly attracted. The new kid in class who was
rumored to have spent time in jail and had been
rehabilitated was *different*. He became mysteri-
ous and fascinating. That pretty girl with dark
hair, who was so good in English and spoke only
when spoken to, was an obvious *contrast* to my
light complexion, my infatuation with football
and my propensity for gab.

We fantasize, most of us, that we are
going to meet the person of our dreams and live
happily ever after. What we do not realize is that
this magical person is going to be different from
us — no matter how many things we have in
common — and that the way we deal with those
differences is what determines whether or not our
relationship is going to work. That pretty girl with
dark hair became my first wife and we made our
differences a constant battleground. Twelve
years after our divorce, I had learned enough
about accepting differences to marry again.
I still chose my opposite, but this time we are
successfully different.

When two people in any relationship are unlike in any way, their encounters can certainly lead to disputes, disagreements and divorce; differences, however, can also provide a relationship with excitement. And why shouldn't they?

When we first meet and are attracted to someone who is different from us, we admire the distinctions. They appeal to us. We are stimulated by someone from whom we get fresh viewpoints on life we might never otherwise experience. Someone different gives us something we don't have, and fills our minds with new possibilities. That is why when you tell me your partner is different from you, and this is causing you problems, I say, hogwash. If you find your partner's differences difficult to deal with, then *you* are the problem. At the very least, you are *part* of the problem.

If you have been spending your time figuring out how to get your partner to change, to see the light, to understand where you are coming from — you have been expending time and energy needlessly. Tell me, in all honesty, that you don't feel you have been on a treadmill, running in circles and getting nowhere. If you want to know how to settle those disputes you've been having at home, let me give you some information that's going to help you. Let me tell you the kinds of differences that most of us encounter and how to deal with them so that you can finally get somewhere with your partner and get a handle on how to enjoy one another — in spite of all these terrible differences you claim are getting in the way.

Kinds of Differences

There are two basic kinds of differences that determine where the rest of our differences lie: personality and environmental.

Personality Differences. These differences, such as personality disorders and neuroses, are emotional problems that people bring into the marriage. They have nothing to do with the marriage itself. They do, however, create problems within the marriage. While healing can be done with partners, these differences are more easily reconciled outside the relationship, in a therapy situation. When you resolve these differences in yourself, then you and your partner can honestly say, "Yes, I want to stay with you" or "No, I do not."

Example...

Power Struggle. Resolving this difference between yourself and your partner means seeing the paradox that when you attempt to have power over another person, that other person is the one who controls the situation. Think about it. Think about the way you are controlled by someone whose actions you feel you must monitor. You must see this by yourself first — perhaps in therapy or counseling — before you work it out with your partner.

Paranoia. Resolving paranoid feelings that arise within your relationship requires that you examine precisely where these feelings are coming from. Your partner may be led to believe that he or she is causing them when in fact you have brought them into the marriage. Your paranoid feelings are best discussed with a therapist who can help you understand their cause and work through the effect they are having on your marriage.

Compulsion/Obsession. We all have our compulsive and obsessive moments — times when we feel we *must* meet a deadline, *must* get to the bank by 1:00 p.m., *can't* get our mind off that new dress or new car and *can't* get to sleep at night. Compulsive and obsessive people, such as hypochondriacs (who are abnormally anxious over their health), bring their imaginary illnesses into their relationships. A marriage can suffer from this obsession and fall apart because of it. This kind of behavior is best treated within a therapy situation.

Environmental Differences. These differences are based on our family origin and upbringing. They are determined by our educational and economic background, age, race, religious beliefs, social status. They also have to do with personal taste and preference, as well as early decisions we made with regard to beliefs and attitudes that are dependent on life experiences. These differences can be reconciled within the relationship itself.

Example...

Environment. You were born, let us say, in a Manhattan tenement, you are the fifth child of six, there was never enough money, you had to work when you were 16 just to help your family survive. Your spouse was brought up in a Southern California house, was an only child, always had the basics, got put through school by parents and did not have to start working until the two of you got married. This is an extreme example. The point is, most of us are attracted to opposites, and these two people, like you and your partner, have differences regarding what life is about.

Education and Philosophy. Your education will directly influence your philosophy and how you look at the world. Someone who has studied and travelled to other parts of the world has had the opportunity to see that some people live differently from others and that one person's way of life is not the only way of life.

Traditional education, or lack thereof, can create diverse reactions to day-to-day situations and can strongly affect your solutions to problems. If, for example, one partner is Asian and one is American, there may be philosophical differences that will affect your life together.

Expectations Based On Beliefs. In Chapter 3, we talked about the games we've played, the myths we all have believed and the ghosts who have invaded our lives and how they have affected our perspective and created certain expectations we have of people and life in general. These will, on many occasions, color a disagreement. If one of you has a tiny mother sitting on your shoulder telling you that you work too hard, and the other of you has a tiny mother saying that you don't work enough — the two of you may well have differences of opinion about what constitutes a normal workday.

The I-Know-Better-Than-You Syndrome.
Perhaps your partner has this attitude — he or she is *right*, and you are judged for your behavior or your belief. Perhaps *you* are this person. Perhaps you have been the one to decide that your partner is *wrong*, and that you are the one who knows better. Think about the times in your life you may have passed judgment on your partner — the times you were absolutely convinced of your being right and hammered your partner with your *rightness*. If you can't think of a time you have done this, ask your partner. He'll know! She'll remember!

The You-Change-So-I-Don't-Have-To Syndrome. Sometimes we want another person to change so that we don't have to. It's as simple as that. Change can be difficult, frustrating, sometimes shattering; we find comfort in staying the same. If I can get you to change your ways, I won't have to change mine.

The truth is that nothing ever stays the same. We are all always changing, and it is self-destructive to believe anything else.

What we are changing into and out of depends on who we are. Sometimes we are changing in order to emerge as our true selves. The sooner we let go of feeling we must be in control, the sooner we become our true selves.

Many of us fall in love and marry at a time when we are growing and changing and have not yet blossomed into the person we finally are by the time we reach, say, the age of 35. Partners of these people sometimes feel deluded by such a change and ask, "Where is the person I married?" They feel robbed, out of control.

Some of us fall into a process of submerging our true selves in order to please others in our lives. This kind of behavior in a partner can be devastating to the relationship as well as to our self, because to be anyone other than your true self is false, painful and destructive. And somewhere down the line, that true self is going to emerge and possibly blow up like Mount Vesuvius, spreading ashes for miles.

The Well-Loved Problem Syndrome.
We all have our well-loved problems
— the ones that keep us from doing
the things we really want to do. They
are the" yeah, but" reasons we
come up with when we are offered
solutions.

Friend: "If you want to lose weight,
you could go to Weight Watchers or
join a gym."

You: "*Yeah, but* I don't have time."

The most common well-loved prob-
lems have to do with health, family, jobs and lack
of education; in hanging on to them, we look for
anything or anyone we can blame, rather than
solve the problem ourselves. Most people with
well-loved problems are produced by families
that pay attention to one another and respect
each other only when there are problems. If you
come from a family like that, take note.

When we hold on to these problems,
we are essentially putting a brick wall between
our partners and ourselves, saying, "We cannot
resolve this."

You: "I have a problem, and it's keeping me from working things out with you."

Friend: "We could talk and work things out together."

You: "*Yeah, but* it won't do any good."

Fear

The common thread that ties all of these difference-producers together is fear. Our fear of the unknown — of what others think of us, of change, of listening to someone else's point of view — often keeps us from resolving differences that could be simply and easily settled. Letting go of fear is a major part of the process of resolving differences. Tell your partner what you are afraid of.

Once you express your fear, you can take the next step — do something about it.

Sexual Differences

Sexual differences can be grave differences in a marriage. They attack the moral fiber in a person and tend to turn into battles beween two distinct attitudes: People-as-things-to-have vs. people-to-be-with. Partners who have a need for pornography, performance demands and dehumanization have a major difference in their marriage from partners who do not, and these differences are not easily re-solved.

Our differences are created when we cancel out new information and refuse to look at each other and listen to what one an-other is saying. If you are guilty of this, you are probably also guilty of not looking at and listen-ing to your own true self.

Looking within your own true self is the only place to begin to resolve your differences.

Differences That Attract; Differences That Repel

Differences are what attract us to each other. Then, once the attraction becomes a union, these very same differences sometimes become unacceptable. We separate because the attractive part of each of us is stymied. What a paradox!

When a relationship starts, we talk about the preferences we have in common, where we have contact. All appearances would confirm that we have the same preferences for lifestyle. After the first year or so, surface images go; real values become more predominant. Both of us had expectations. Then, we are no longer certain we have the same purposes. The choice then is to take a stand, or integrate differences.

When we begin to accept our *self* for who we truly are, accept our loved ones for who they are, and accept that although we often experience different truths, no one is right and no one is wrong — we are better able to reconcile our differences. This takes communication.

Being intimate with someone is coming into contact with that person's differences.

Facing our differences and learning to accept them is what makes our differences successful.

We will never be accepted as we want to be accepted as long as we present an image of ourselves that is not true. We defeat our relationships when we are indifferent to who the people in our relationships are. Many of our differences are really nothing more than personal taste, like color preference. I like blue and you like green. How do we reconcile this?

Differences are not disagreements until we make them so. Sometimes people say things differently than we expect, and we assume them to be contradictory when they are not. When we demand that *contradictory* differences be submerged, we lose the spark and energy that differences bring us and we generate more misconceptions. The energy-draining process of black-white, right-wrong thinking inhibits our accepting differences.

Dealing With Differences

In order to begin dealing with differences between you and your partner, you are going to have to take on an attitude you may have never considered before. It's one of those 180° turns we've been talking about. In a relationship, nobody wins unless both sides win. Resolving differences requires that partners win together.

Pam and Ted

Pam met Ted when she was 25. She was an English teacher at a university and had spent most of her life around quiet, conservative people. Ted was different. He was as intelligent and well educated as she; at the same time he was outspoken, aggressive, confident, and he knew how to make friends quickly and get things done. Pam was utterly intrigued. He was powerful and certain, and she was excited by him. He presented her with a world full of new opportunities. Pam and Ted spent every free moment together, talking about their likes and dislikes, their hopes and dreams.

It fascinated Ted that Pam could get so much out of the simple act of watching the sun set. He loved the way she put the world aside, as if it didn't matter, and drank in the beauty of something so natural and common that happened every day. Pam was amazed that Ted could announce he was going to do something and just do it, without concern that maybe he wouldn't be able to. He announced that he was going to retire a wealthy man at the age of 40, and she believed this was true.

Ted and Pam got married. It wasn't long before Pam began to find Ted's aggressiveness disturbing. He was always firm about getting the attention he wanted. In a restaurant, he would sometimes loudly hit his glass of water with a knife; at a movie, he would get his tickets and bypass everyone in line. Among friends, he talked a lot and told many stories, sometimes never bringing Pam into the conversation. Sometimes he forthrightly put people down. Pam began to apologize for him, correct him, not feel good about him.

Ted began to feel that Pam was becoming critical of him, that he was growing less comfortable with being who he was when she was around. He also began to feel that she was never going to get anywhere in her career because she

didn't speak up for herself. He began to accuse her of not taking
charge of her life.

The very differences which had
attracted these people to one another became
the battleground of their marriage. It happens
often. But why?

How could someone who intrigues us
and excites us become someone
who embarrasses us — someone we
want to change?

If we once saw our mate's differences as exciting and attractive,
why do we now see them as contrary and frustrating?

How do we suddenly get to a place
and time when our point of view is
right and our mate's point of view is
wrong?

When do acceptance and love turn
into judgment and evaluation?

Remember the myths we discussed
in Chapter 3 — the ones we all believe, the ones

that plague us throughout our lives? Pam believed that if Ted "really loved her," he would change his outspoken behavior. Ted believed that if Pam would just "do what he said," she would see that he was right.

How could Pam expect Ted to not be outspoken when he has been outspoken all his life? Furthermore, his outspokenness was something she loved and was attracted to when she first met him. And what brought Ted to the conclusion that Pam would be better off if she became more like him? Didn't he fall in love with her because she was different from him? Did he really believe that making her over into his own image was going to make things better?

The answer is yes. That's what he thought. You and I do this every day. We want people to change for us. We want the food checker to not be so friendly to people ahead of us so we can get through the check-out line faster. We want our employees to do things our way, even if they can still get the job done their way — more efficiently. We want our employers to understand when we need a day off, even though they have an important business venture going on. We want our children to behave the way we want them to, and we want our spouses to think more like we do, act more like we do and be more like we are so that we can feel more sure that who we are is okay, and right, and good.

Acknowledge Your Differences

The first step in reconciling their differences is for Ted and Pam to acknowledge that they have them — to themselves and to one another. And you must do the same. Let your partner know that you are aware of the differences between you — that you have them, that he or she has them — and that you honestly want to work them out. If only one of you is ready to acknowledge your differences and open to talking, the process cannot begin. Chances are that if you truly want to work them out and you say so, your partner will, at least, listen.

Regard Your Partner's Economy of Self

Remember when we discussed earlier how we all started life needing to do nothing more than *be* in order to be loved? Start there. Look at your partner as someone who does not have to do anything more than *be* in order for you to show him or her your love. I know this may not be easy. It is, however, time for you to do something different from what you have been doing, because what you have been doing has not been working.

Rather than thinking about all those attributes and attitudes you would like to change, fix or improve in your partner, focus on those that simply *are*, and do your best to re-move all judgment from them. Rather than, "I wish he didn't...." or "She'd be better off if she didn't...." look at him as he is; accept her as she is. She is hyper. He does smoke. She does inter-rupt you when you're reading or watching the game on TV. He does love to watch football on sunny beach days. He does; he is. She does; she is.

This is someone you love, and true love is allowing a person to be exactly who he or she is and giving that person room to be, to grow, to change in order to become all that he or she can be. If you have never done this be-fore, the process may not come easy. Once you get the knack of it, however, you will not want to be any other way. What is required is a change in thinking — *your* thinking. The one and only truth in this situation is the one that follows, and you will need to remember it when you are working on developing your regard for your partner's true self:

The only change possible is the one you decide to make in your own thinking.

Either you will respect your partner, with all his or her beliefs and views of the world, or you will not. Either you will see that everyone has the right to be respected for who they are, or you will not. Love is a decision.

Joan and Steve

Joan wanted certain changes made in the landscaping of the new home she and Steve bought. The two of them disagreed about what should be done. Steve felt that Joan was, once again, manipulating him. He felt that there was no area in their relationship in which Joan simply let him be, where he could work on a project without her "advice." He deeply resented this.

They discussed this and made an agreement that the outside of the house would be Steve's province, and the inside of the house would be Joan's.

It wasn't long before Joan was making comments about how she thought the landscape should look. She wasn't intentionally avoiding their agreement. She simply had not made a change in her own thinking. Her mother had always criticized her father, and this simply was behavior she had learned and adopted and never stopped to think about. But when Steve became angrier than he'd ever been, she started to think.

She had never trusted him to do the job on his own. She had never trusted him to do anything without voicing an opinion. It reminded Steve of being in school and being criticized by teachers for not drawing his picture correctly. To Steve there was no right or wrong about drawing a picture, and there is no right or wrong about how to do a garden — gardening involves crea-

tive decisions and, therefore, is totally subjective.

Joan was advised to think about
Steve as a creative man, with a
certain competence, personal taste
and perception, whose judgment
may not agree with hers yet whose
opinions were certainly valuable and
acceptable. She practiced thinking
about him in this way. Before long,
when she showed friends around the
grounds of their new home, she
began to brag about what a wonderful job Steve was doing. She
praised his color combinations and
landscape design. Every time she
wanted to change something in the
garden, she looked at Steve and
concentrated on putting herself in
his shoes, thinking about how she
would feel being criticized for her
creativity.

She loved Steve and gave him the
room to be who he is. And in time —
the fascinating outcome that often
follows — he came to request her
opinions and found within himself the

ability to accept her suggestions without looking upon them as criticism. The ultimate act that led to making their differences successful occurred when they began to joke about Joan's uninvited opinions and Steve's landscape ego.

Steve: "I don't suppose you'd have an *opinion* on which new plants to put in this year."

Joan: "Me? Why, you know I don't know a *thing* about design. Aside from the fact that I adore white roses, thrill to the scent of jasmine and positively swoon at the sight of kalanchoe — no, no opinion."

Discuss Why You Want Your Partner To Change

For starters, talk to your partner. Say, "I want you to change, because....." You fill in the blank. Maybe you need more than one blank. You can start off by acknowledging that you want your partner to change so you won't have to. Perhaps you can both have a good laugh about that. Humor is essential to good communication between partners, and resolution of differences can be hastened by it. Here are samples to start you off. You can take turns filling them in.

> I want you to change the way you dress/cook/think/act so I don't have to change the way I feel about the way you dress/cook/think/act.
>
> I want you to change, because I get angry when you...
>
> I want you to change the way you...
>
> I think you would be better off if you...
>
> The reason I want you to make this change is...
>
> I want you to be more...
>
> I want you to be less ...

I am sure you can come up with many more — your own reasons for wanting your partner to change. When you have had enough of these and have, hopefully, reached a point of laughter after working through the tough ones, take turns saying this to each other:

> **"Don't change anything about your-self. I love you exactly the way you are."**

When you've completed this exercise and you have been able to say this last statement to one another, think about how you feel after saying it. Is it a feeling you're going to want to have again?

Focus On What's Right, Rather Than On What's Wrong

We must take a new approach to differences. We must not seek to eliminate them. We must seek to reconcile them. Differences must find fertile soil to grow in.

We learn from differences. The most contradictory truths do not necessarily have to compete with, or dominate, each other — they can simply stand side by side.

In accepting the differences between us, we create new connections; and

**this effort alone, to find and make
those connections, erases the differences that divide us.**

Focus on what's right. Start by telling
one another what works well in your relationship.
Tell your partner the things you truly love about
her or him.

Focus on what's good about your
differences — the ones that attracted you to
each other in the first place. You say your partner is too aggressive. Think about what's positive
about that aggressiveness and tell your partner.
You say your partner is too submissive. Tell your
partner some positive aspects you see in his or
her submissive behavior.

Example...

"I have wanted you to dress up
more, because I feel that by dressing
up you present yourself in the best
possible light. I see, however, that
you enjoy comfort, and that when
you dress comfortably, you are happier, and when you're happy, you
look good.

"The Queen of England, however, is

coming to dinner tomorrow night, so do you think you'd survive not wearing blue jeans for just one night?"

Example...

"I have wanted you to change, because I get angry every time you tell me not to salt my food. I feel like a child who is being mothered. When you tell me I should not salt my food, I see, however, that your reasons could involve an interest in my health."

"When I reach for the salt shaker, however, it's a choice I've made as an adult person. I know how you feel about my using salt. You don't have to say a word."

Example...

"I've wanted you to be less money-conscious. Yet I see that by being concerned about money, you make sure we are taken care of, and I appreciate that. (Pause.) Could you loan me a couple thousand 'til Tuesday?"

Deal With Solutions Instead of Problems

We are besieged by would-be cures that don't do anything. Even more problems arise when we do not go about dealing with our difficulties in a way that will be beneficial to us. When we attempt to fix or change the symptoms of a problem, we fail to solve anything. The problem merely takes on new symptoms. We make marriage "the problem." The truth is that marriage is not the problem. *We* are the problem, and the solution is to look at your *self* and my *self*.

In dealing with solutions, rather than problems, we do not say, "I should have said" or "I should have done" something differently. This focus on the past solves nothing. Focus on what you want and how you feel *now*:

Example...

I have wanted you to change the way you dress.

I feel upset when you do this.

The reason I feel this way is I used to get punished for not dressing

properly. I feel the way you're dressing will reflect on me.

After you've talked this out, ask one
another: **"How can we resolve this?"**

Example...

I've wanted you to change the way
you talk to the children.

I feel scared when you talk to them
the way you do.

It makes me think of when I was a
child and my father beat me when
he was angry.

Then, after you've discussed this, ask
for assistance: **"Help me. How do we make this
work?"**

The idea here is to state why you
have wanted your partner to change, how this
makes you feel, and most important, rather than
accusing your partner of any wrongful behavior,
explain why you, yourself, are upset by this behavior. To handle your differences with another
person, you must be in contact with your own
essence, your own truth.

Instead of:
"**You were wrong** to scold the children,"

you say:
"**I feel** scared when you scold the children, **because** I get scared you'll hurt them."

Have you ever talked with someone who is not satisfied with the way you are, who has a secret or not-so-secret program to change you? How did this make you feel? Did you really make contact with that person? Did you communicate? No. Because that person was talking to the person he or she thought you were, or should be, and you were busy resisting the person that he or she was imagining you to be. What a lot of hard work! And for what? No communication!

When you deal with solutions instead of problems, you state the facts, without any judgments. Notice the distinction between the two following statements made by Joan:

"Steve likes to play golf more than I do. I'd rather work in my garden."

"Steve is foolish for spending so much time on the golf course. He could be doing something constructive, like gardening, instead."

You get the same information about Steve and Joan. In the second statement, however, you also get Joan's judgment.

Talk to your partner about certain words that trigger your feeling judged — like "foolish" and "crazy" and "you could be doing something constructive." Sometimes one simple word will create conflict and build into a monstrous argument.

Accept One Another's Differences

Accepting one another's differences is the most natural thing in the world. Our relationships are our own creations, and we can make them into anything we desire. We must accept that our relationships are the way they are, because we have caused them to be that way. In accepting this, we can accept, therefore, that if we do not like them the way they are, we can change them.

The point is not whether we make right choices or wrong choices. The point is that we make choices. The point is not that we love too much or too little, too long or too short. The point is that we love. We make choices and we love based on who we are, what we want, what we are feeling and what we need at the time. These are all variables that change from day to day, sometimes from moment to moment.

Ask yourself these questions and take time to think of your honest reply:

How am I different from my partner?

What do I do with these differences?

Do I change or fix my partner?

Do I minimize the differences?

Am I disappointed with the differences?

What is the process I use when I want to change my partner?

What happens when I work at changing my partner?

Now, ask these questions and take the time you need to respond truthfully:

What can I say to accept my partner's differences?

What actions can I take to show my partner I accept his/her differences?

Do I love my partner enough to let her/him be different?

How do I feel simply letting him/her *be*?

The following questions ask you to take a close look at how you and your partner function together:

When you and your partner talk, plan, work out the details of your daily life...

Is it a positive process?

Is it a negative process?

Do you invariably wind up fighting?

Are you able to divide responsibilities and work toward a goal?

When something bothers you about
your partner's behavior, do you
keep it inside, or are you able to say
something?

Do you deny your differences, hop-
ing that they will disappear?

Working toward the success of your
relationship means accepting your differences,
talking about differences you cannot accept,
and doing something about the differences you
find unacceptable.

**A successful relationship means
growth of both individuals as well as
growth of the unification of those
individuals.**

The Turning Point

We have discussed many turning
points in this chapter. Look at them and see
which ones might be necessary to help you out
of the stuck place you are in right now:

Playing games gives you the exact
opposite of what you want. If you
are getting nowhere in your attempt

to get what you want, take a 180°
turn. Decide what you really want
and ask for it.

Relationships are different from sports
in that both sides can win. Take the
180° turn and look at the ways both
you and your partner can get what
you want.

If you believe there is a quick fix for
your problems, take the 180° turn,
unequivocally accept that there is
no quick fix, and take more appropriate, long-term steps.

If you have always believed that
confrontation is harmful and frightening, believe that it is in the best interest of your relationship, and give it a
shot.

If you have always believed that you
must rebel in order to maintain your
strength, just for the sake of opting
for something new — don't rebel. If
you are asked to come home at
7:30, decide to get home at 7:30,
willingly. See how you feel.

If you have grown up believing that confrontations turn into battles, decide right now that you will discuss your problem *before* a battle erupts.

If you have felt afraid that every time you speak from your heart, you lose power — do it. Speak from your heart and see the power you wield.

If you have always believed that confronting issues is committing aggression, believe for awhile that confrontation is actually saying "I care about you." It really is, you know.

Instead of seeing your differences as "You vs. Me," have a look at what you can do with "How Can *We* Work This Out."

If you have been blaming your partner for not coming through for you, let go of your blame. Take the 180° turn and look at what you yourself are afraid of. Ask yourself what scares you about what your partner is doing.

Talk about your games, your myths and misconceptions, and the ghosts that still haunt your lives — and please, for yourself — get out of your stuck place — do something different. It could be *your* turning point.

To heal suffering, sometimes we must turn and open to it, because the only alternative is more pain. If you are getting nowhere in your attempt to get what you want, look at the ways both you and and your partner can get what you want — together. We do not have to be reassured or rescued from our distressing feelings. We have to be allowed to go through our pain so we have the experience of knowing that we can survive and grow.

If you like blue and your partner likes green, I'm sure you would never put much effort into insisting that your partner like blue. If you bought your partner a present, I think you would buy green. The next time your partner does or says something you consider a *difference* between you, accept the point of view as being him or her. Give your partner a present — and make it green. See what happens.

Differences

6

THE STRUGGLE

We struggle with the lies we've lived with and attempt to make them truth.

—*The Paradox of Struggle*

You may feel that happiness is owed to you by the Universe, or at least by the Bill of Rights. I may feel certain the Bill of Rights ensures me a right to happiness. You and I may not have noticed that the phrase "*pursuit* of happiness" places the responsibility on us. By demanding to *have* happiness, we don't have a chance to *be* happy. The reason? The very process of demanding to have something engages us in a struggle.

Every one of us in a relationship has struggles within ourselves as well as with our partners. We either reconcile these struggles, we compromise, give up, batter the other (mentally, emotionally or physically), or in some way erode the foundation of our relationship. A serious struggle can destroy the sturdiest foundation, whether based on loving essence-to-essence contact or on each person's conditioning — maybe even on a combination of the two.

When we look at any situation in terms of who is right and who is wrong, rather than how to make the situation work for both of us, only one can *win* — and in that case, both *sides* lose. Most disagreements today have winners and losers because we bring ideas of what is right and wrong into a relationship in which there is no right or wrong. Once we find a resolution in which both parties gain, then we begin to make progress.

doesn't love Josie.

This could be new information for
Josie. Perhaps she has been interpreting his
reading or computing after making love as a
sign that he does not love her. If she cancels out
this new information instead of accepting and

integrating it, she has a great deal of investment
in being *right* and she will not open to the
thoughts and feelings she will need for them to
reconcile their differences. By not accepting
Jim's night-owlishness, Josie does not accept
who Jim is.

The Quest For The "Perfect" Life

Nobody gets married thinking of
getting divorced. Yet, divorce happens. Many
of life's struggles and conflicts are not of our own
making — a death in the family, the loss of a job.
Those that are of our own making often come
from our "well-loved" problems — the ones we
create for ourselves out of some notion about
how life *should* be, *could* be, *better* be.

> Georgia left college during the De-
> pression because her husband said
> they didn't have enough money.
> Several years later, when her hus-
> band got money, he bought a truck
> for his business rather than helping
> her go back to college. Now in her
> 40s, Georgia feels her husband
> *should have* given her money to
> return to college. She says she has
> wasted her life.

Georgia's quest for the perfect life was in being *the perfect wife*. She gave herself away to be fulfilled and wound up disappointed. She tells this story often. It's one of her well-loved problems that she tells with relish, because it seems to give her a sense of importance, a sense of having had to struggle, a sense of martyrdom. Her husband says she can go back to college any time she wants to, and he leaves the room every time she tells the tale.

The Absurdity of The Struggle

If we do not recognize and acknowledge one another's real self, then we're caught in the spiral of doing the same thing over and over again, and having to struggle more and get less. When we can accept that there's truth in your statement and truth in my statment, then we can see that the struggle is absurd. We can then laugh over the fact that we got into this ridiculous struggle in the first place.

The more we struggle with a quest for the perfect life, the more need we feel and the less satisfaction we get. The struggle controls us. The question to ask is: How did we get into this struggle? And, more important, what are we going to do about it *now*?

Where Do Struggles Come From?

If you know you are struggling in your relationship, yet you aren't sure what the struggle is about, here are some suggestions. Major struggles come from:

Wanting to change your partner's difference.

Wanting to change yourself to meet your partner's needs.

Competing with your partner.

Taking on family, inlaw and society standards.

Attempting to be just like your partner.

Being dependent rather than inter-dependent.

Expecting therapy to fix your partner.

Honoring each other's pretensions.

Creating surface change.

Bringing individual inner conflicts into the union.

How Can We Reconcile The Struggles?

If you've spotted the ones that apply to you, know that you can stop struggling provided you are *both* willing to work. When one partner is willing and one is not, reconciliation usually means separation.

Reconciliation and staying together depend on:

Identifying the conflicts.

Stopping the games.

Accepting one another's differences.

Accepting imperfections in spouse and marriage.

Confronting what is okay and not okay.

Contacting what is available here and now.

Taking a look at yourself.

If you are truly interested in reconciling your partnership, you have a better chance of reconciliation if you begin by suggesting ways to honestly change yourself.

Demands and Defenses

Demands on your partner and defenses of your own behavior undermine love. The following demands/defenses sometimes run deep inside us and we don't always see that they are what's getting in the way of reconciling our differences:

Have No Expectations. If you expect nothing of yourself, you won't feel you've failed at anything. This is a defense that protects you from feelings of joy over your accomplishments and those of others. It ensures that you will have no ability to direct and shape your future.

Make No Commitments. This defense reflects fear of asking for what we want; a low level of self-esteem that says you'll never get what you want anyway, and leaves no fertile ground in which a relationship can take root and grow.

Don't Ask For What You Want. If they really love you, they should know. Insisting that others be mind readers, and never exposing your wants, defends you from disappointment; you can then blame the other person when you don't get what you want.

Insist That Sex Be Wonderful All The Time. Like it's *supposed to be*. By maintaining this fantasy, we can completely disconnect from the other person's needs, state of being or ability to give, as well as our own.

Insist On Maintaining A 50/50 Relationship. There is no way for two people to measure their contributions equally. Insisting on this kind of relationship is the opposite of love because there is no caring about the satisfaction or security of the other person.

Never Expose Your True Feelings. Never allow yourself to be vulnerable. Maintaining facades and illusions, except to strike out in anger or manipulation, guarantees that no one will ever get close enough to hurt you, or love you.

Never Take What's Offered As A Gift.
We sometimes fear givers, because we don't
know what the rules are and where the strings are.
The only people comfortable around a giver are
those who can manipulate the giver, or feel comfortable enough within themselves to be able to
receive without feeling guilty.

Demanding More Than What's Available

Power. Once someone gets a sense
of power over someone else, abuse is hard to
resist. Paradoxically, the one who supposedly
has that power loses a sense of self as a dignified
human being; sooner or later a symptom of
grave discontent appears, because someone is
living a lie. Real power lies in truth.

No one will change until their need
for change is greater than their need to stay
where they are. Help from a partner is not trusted
because the first person's place, dignity, responsibilities, and accountability of self have not been
clear or straight from the beginning.

Neediness. Both forms of neediness — total independence and total clinging — are detrimental to marriages. They both demand more than what is available. The one who needs to be super independent, male or female, has about as much empathy for the dependent one as a triathlete has for a fumble foot. Often one keeps getting needier, as the other keeps rejecting and setting up barriers.

Over The Edge

One more drink
One more overdrawn checkbook
One more late night at the office
One more baby
One more club to join
One more weekend with the inlaws
One more junked car in the yard

These are all bottom lines that have put relationships over the edge. They come as a result of constant behavior that does not change. The bottom line erupts when there has been continual demand for more than what is available until finally, that last straw breaks the camel's back.

The Struggle

7

TRUTH, TRUST AND INTIMACY

Our relationship grows more intimate when we accept our differences, not when we become the same.

—The Paradox of Intimacy

The Feeling of Truth

When I'm talking to someone at a party, and I don't feel good about myself when I walk away, that feeling serves as a red flag that I've been false with that person. I know I didn't confront or at least set straight what my limits were, what's acceptable and not acceptable to me; or I was false to myself by presenting an image I thought the person would approve of.

When we walk away from an encounter feeling bad, we've been in a game in which there was no contact. Where there is no truth, there is no contact. When we acknowledge our differences, however, we've made an incredible, intimate contact. Our relationship grows from expanding to accept the ways we are different, not from becoming more alike.

We don't ever have to second-guess each other when we tell the truth. We can detach ourselves from our demands about that other, and give up the safety of being in control. And we do not have to give up romantic love in the process. Truth and clarity do not preclude romance.

The Importance of Trust

We sometimes talk about the importance of trust in a relationship. I have to trust you; you have to trust me. What does this mean? What have we got when we trust each other?

I see trust as a kind of safety. I feel safe being who I am in front of you; and you feel safe with me. Ideally, we know we can tell each other what we want, share our thoughts and feelings and learn from one another. There are two kinds of safety:

Trust No One: People who don't trust anyone, including themselves, find safety in defending and protecting themselves from true contact. They don't allow their true feelings to emerge. When a feeling does surface, it manifests itself as hysteria rather than as a true feeling. Even joy shows up in a hysterical manner.

Trust Yourself: When you trust yourself, you find safety in trusting others. You know that you are capable of acting in your own best interests while dealing with other people's interests. You know, in essence, that you are safe, no matter what.

Everyone in a relationship needs a safety zone within that relationship — a place to retreat where there are no attacks or put-downs. This is a demilitarized zone. Couples need to agree that each can call a time-out if a discussion gets so emotionally hot that they've lost what they started talking about. One person can stop a confrontation by saying, "I need some safety from this right now. It's too much for me *right now.*" When you trust one another, you can allow each other this kind of safe place.

It's better to call a time-out con- sciously and with agreement rather than go away and hide. If we all had safety zones, per- haps there would be less of a need for alcohol, drugs, TV, sickness and all the other defenses we use in our system. People who have learned economy of self can claim their own safety. They instinctively know when they need to be in this safety zone, and they announce their need and spend time there.

When you are in emotional pain, and someone really listens to you and com- pletely hears what you say, the emotional charge and need to be heard is taken care of, regardless of whether or not you agree with that person's response to your pain. That's why it's important to say what's on your mind, and to be honest when you are not in a place where you can listen. Listening, with ears, mind and soul truly open is one of the greatest gifts you can give.

Trusting Yourself

The best way to feel good about revealing your differences is to feel good about yourself — to trust yourself. In order to do this, you must make contact with your self, get close to your self, get to know your self. This focusing on self is not a closing off — not what people sometimes call "selfish" in a derogatory way. Rather, it is an opening up. You open your mind and your heart to who you are. You get to know yourself the way you would want to get to know a best friend. You trust that you are not going to harm yourself, or give yourself up and that you are going to accept yourself as you are.

While you may see your potential to become a wiser, more caring, sensitive person, you know from the beginning that who you are is good.

Once you are able to accept this in yourself, you are then able to accept this in your partner and others. Once you trust that you will not harm your self, you can trust that you will not harm your partner. Once your partner trusts him or her self, he/she can trust that he/she will not harm you. At this point of trust between you, you can look at one another's differences and accept them for what they are. At this point, you are ready for intimacy.

The Comfort of Intimacy

Pete and Annie were in the middle of the Menomini Indian reservation, in the wilderness, and Annie said, "Pete, we're lost!" Pete said, "No, Annie, as of this moment in time, we are where we are."

Intimacy is contacting the essence or truth of another person — including that person's difference — and seeing: "Here is where she is *right now*. Maybe this is not where she wants to be, or where I'd like her to be. The fact is — this is where she is." It's seeing that: "He's struggling through this problem right now; he feels lost. That's why he's such a terror to live with. I wish he'd change. But he can't right now. This is where he is, and, for now, I have to accept this."

Trust is the essence of intimacy.

The belief that we cannot enjoy each other *until* we understand each other destroys most relationships before they begin. We must trust that even though we don't understand our partner, that he or she has good reasons for his/her actions. The only thing we need to under-stand is that we *don't* understand.

We make contact with our partners when no expectations of them get in the way.

When you are not willing to contact intimately — when you feel this is too great a risk — you are succumbing to fears you might have had as a child, or as a young adult, when you were free to be intimate and might have gotten hurt. If you are aware of this, you will understand that this could be depriving you of charity, gener-osity and a sense of humor.

Jo Ann's Fear

Involvement scares Jo Ann. She prefers to remain *safe*. But her safety gets her nothing; therefore, she gets needy and greedy, wants more, and places greater demands on those around her.

Jo Ann does not develop significant relationships, although she spends a great deal of energy looking for "Mr. Right." She lives in a narcissistic bubble. Until she can expand her sense of *I* to her sense of *We*, she won't have a significant involvement with a man. She has a long list of things a man will do if he loves her. Deciding how the relationship should be is her safety zone and keeps her in control, at the cost of making no contact. She attempts to change a man to fit how she thinks he should be. She makes no contact, gets little out of relating, and therefore demands more.

In order to get what she really wants, she will have to give up her expectations, the safety of being in control, and quit working so hard to get involved.

Once she gives up her expectations, she will be more likely to fulfill them.

8

CONFRONTATION
AND CHANGE

By rejecting the role of change agent, we make change possible.

—*The Paradox of Change.*

When should you confront your partner? Whenever the need is there. Even though confrontation can be painful, the sooner an issue is brought up, the less chance there is for resentment to build up and truth to be lost. Letting an issue build up in your mind tends to place your focus on being *right* instead of on the truth.

It's good for couples to sit down every year, every 5, 10 or 20 years, to re-evaluate their relationship and re-contract their marriages: Where are we okay? Where are we not okay? Most of us re-evaluate only in crisis situations — when someone wants a divorce, someone wants to separate, someone is unfaithful and is found out. Why wait that long? Why not re-evaluate before a breakdown in communication? Why not talk now before it's too late?

Confrontation is in your best interest. In the act of confrontation, you take care of your self and your partner's self. You create positive, forward-moving energy to solve problems. Energy going forward does not have to be violent; nor does it have to disregard others' needs. Bottom-line confrontation nips a problem in the bud, without blame, before a head of steam develops under it —before Mt. Vesuvius erupts, burying your marriage like Pompeii.

Marriages that sometimes appear to be the worst, most confrontive ones are often the best, because they are up-front.

The essence of relationships is intimacy and is based on confronting something that's not feeling comfortable or clear between two people. Intimacy is saying what is the truth for you. It means, "I care enough about you and about us to open these issues and deal with them — now."

Either make contact, or live a very deprived life. When you make contact, you expand. Your center comes back, not to the original place but to some place in between the expansion and where you started. Confrontation does this. We often think of confrontation as aggression, but confrontation has nothing to do with aggression. To confront is to state a difference, draw a boundary. Once the difference is accepted, the confrontation melts.

Change means to make or become different. Some of us find change difficult, because change scares us. It implies a loss of permanence, a psychological risk, possible danger and adjustments to people and places in our lives to which we are accustomed. Changing the way you and your partner relate to one another after many years of marriage can appear to be impossible.

When we think of *change*, many of us envision a drastic change. If we've been not relating at all, we feel we must relate all the time. The best program for change, however, begins at the one-foot end of the swimming pool and takes whatever time is necessary to get to the 10-foot end. To make changes in a relationship, we have to look back, step by step, at what happened, how it began to self-destruct, and how we can change that. It takes time to look at what each of us was doing and how our actions affected the other. Sometimes we discover we were doing well, and past experiences got in our way. Sometimes we find we were not doing well, even though our heart was in the right place.

Reframing

Reframing an old picture can often give it new life. When we reframe a relationship, the same thing can happen. Reframing our problem is re-interpreting it — perhaps taking a 180° turn, doing the opposite of what we did at first. The new frame of reference has a positive connotation. For example, *fear* is re-labeled *excitement; confusion* is re-labeled *process-toward-growth.*

You may laugh and ask, "How can something that terrifies me turn into something that excites me?" The answer is: perspective. The image of the 8-ounce drinking glass that contains 4 ounces of water is a good example. Is the glass half-empty? Or half-full? Martha Washington is credited with having said, "The greater part of our happiness or misery depends on our dispositions and not our circumstances." What's your disposition like today? How is it affecting decisions you're making and actions you're taking?

Tom Sawyer reframed whitewashing a fence, treating the chore as something to be enjoyed rather than dreaded. Soon his friends were asking to be allowed to work the fence too. In Shakespeare's "The Taming of the Shrew," Petruchio knows that Katherine will reject food and shelter he will provide, so he villifies them before she can reject them. He thereby succeeds in getting her to accept them. He counts on her contradicting him and accomplishes his purpose by stating the opposite of what he intended. Sometimes you have to be tough to be loving.

Your perception of any situation can change. By turning and seeing yourself and your partner from a different perspective, deep, permanent change can begin to take place. I remarked to a fighting couple that they must really be deeply, emotionally involved to fight with one another the way they do. They thought about that and stopped arguing to prove me wrong!

We fight change as if it were the plague when the truth is, everything, everywhere is constantly changing.

When change is put into a paradoxical framework, so that we see the absurdity and humor of our problems, growth begins to take place. Let's take a closer look at change.

First Order Change [1]

First order change is the kind we make when we rearrange furniture, step on the accelerator of a car, or say we will remember to replace the toothpaste cap when we're finished using the toothpaste. It occurs *within* a given system. For example, a couple having relationship problems purchases a new home or has a baby to break the stagnation in their relationship. First order change always looks like a common sense move.

First order change is an *intention* to make a change in behavior. "You want me to not criticize you; okay, I won't." Joan said she would change and wouldn't criticize Steve. Then she did. Her original promise was made only to appease Steve. First order change is generally not a permanent change, nor one that requires you to let go of anything. You say you will change, to ease the tension of the moment. You don't necessarily follow up on your promise.

Second Order Change [1]

Second order change is a major change. While first order change is a change in the system, in second order change the system itself changes. Rather than moving the furniture around, we get rid of the furniture and buy new furniture. Rather than stepping on the accelerator of your car, you sell your sports car and buy a stationwagon. You move from a five-bedroom house on five acres of land into a condo; or you start your own business after spending 10 years as someone's assistant. Second order change means adopting new attitudes or behavior. You intend to change, and you take responsibility for making your intention a reality. Second order change often looks like anything *but* common sense. It is, however, long-term.

When Joan agreed to see Steve as a man of certain abilities and sensitivities, especially with regard to garden landscaping — someone she wanted to be happy — she was able to make a second order change. She stepped into Steve's shoes, saw how he felt and decided that her behavior was adversely affecting Steve. This made her *want* to make a change.

Second order change is roses on her birthday, because *she* loves them; or Superbowl tickets for his, because *he* loves football. This is everyday, what-life-is-all-about stuff. Second order change is seeing the garage door left open, thinking about the absurdity of getting upset about an open garage door, and closing it yourself. Second order change is an attitude change. It is a simple acceptance of the fact that we can change ourselves, if we want to.

Jan and Tom

Jan knew, and wouldn't admit she knew, that Tom was having an affair. She complained about his late hours and calls at home from his secretary. Finally they had a showdown. Tom agreed to replace his secretary "within a few months." On Tom's part, this was obviously a first order change.

Jan's insecurity continued to mount because she knew Tom had not changed the attitude that allowed for his infidelity. Jan decided to enroll in a career training program.

You may not see this as a resolution to the problem of having an unfaithful husband; however, Jan's decision was a second order change. Because she saw the absurdity of Tom requesting a few more months with this secretary, she decided to get on with the rest of her life, preparing to take care of herself and her family. Tom can now change his attitude and be loyal to his family, or he can decide not to. Jan understands that she has no control over his choice; she can only take care of herself. She is willing to maintain the marriage under certain conditions; however, her life is not hostage to the marriage or to Tom's whims. She has become free of his problem.

Change occurs when people become who they are, not when they attempt to be what they are not. You don't have to justify your life to anyone. This is your life. When you stop striving for the impossibility of an image of perfection, when you stop attempting to become what you are not and accept yourself, then you will change.

Rather than spending your life fighting who you are, you can relax and say, "Okay, this is who I am. Where can I go from here?" Change, in its simplest form, is accepting your own way of being.

Your Change Creates Other Changes

Those of us seeking change are caught in a war between what we are and what we think we should be, never fully identifying with either.

True change is possible only when we let go of what we think we should be, and experience who we are.

Once we take this step, we are different. And, being different, we have an effect on those people in our lives with whom we are in constant contact.

Change in one person within a system affects all the others. Change has a rippling effect — the kind you see when you throw a stone into a body of water. When that stone hits the water, the water ripples out in several directions, changing the water. When you change to take care of yourself, other changes will take place. You can count on it.

The only person you can possibly change is you. If you find this a frightening prospect, you are not alone. Having to change your self in order to be happy puts all of the responsibility back on you. It means no more blaming others for your unhappiness. No more using an "unhappy childhood" as an excuse for not taking action. No more accusing dictatorial parents for causing you to be weak today. Sometimes, when we change ourselves, others in our lives find the need to change as well. Sometimes. I *still* close the garage door.

[1] As described in *Change* by Paul Watzlawick, Ph.D., John Weakland, Ch.E., and Richard Fisch, M.D.

9

ACCEPTANCE

Your true self is the old self you wanted to run away from in the beginning.

—The Paradox of Self Acceptance

When I accept you, I don't put any energy into changing you. Then I begin to appreciate you. If I resent you, how on earth am I going to be able to appreciate you as you are?

When we find in ourselves that place

in which we accept the other person, some amazing things begin to happen. For example, we no longer need to control the other to defend our illusions of ourselves. The manipulation is over. We let go of the myths, we stop playing the games, and we merely live. Acceptance is saying, "I love the way I love." I don't accuse myself of loving *too much* or *not enough*. I simply acknowledge that this is how I love.

Acceptance is looking at life in a positive way. It is asking, "How are *we* going to do this?" rather than "Why aren't *you* doing that?" A positive question will get us a positive answer. Positive thinking leads to positive actions. Whatever we think and feel always comes out in the actions we take.

There is so much to accept in one another as time goes by. As we get older, we have to accept that we are aging. If we haven't accepted ourselves and one another now, we're going to have trouble accepting ourselves as older. With aging comes a change in attitudes, habits, sexual behavior. Accepting that you've had 10, 20, 30 or more good years together will enable you to accept that maybe there are going to be fewer orgasms.

Acceptance means seeing that you have enough to be happy. I know a man named John, whose wife Jane wants a divorce. John would give Jane a divorce except for the fact that he's got $4.5 million and he doesn't want to have to give her half. The interest on half ($2.25 million) at 5% is about $112,500 a year! What more does John want? When is enough enough?

Sense of Humor

Dealing with differences with a sense of humor is going to make all the difference in the world to your relationship. When you can laugh at one another's *faults* and see the kinds of things you do that have an effect on your partner, you find solutions quickly, and acceptance becomes easy. Laughter *is* one of the first solutions.

Josie and Jim

Josie wanted to buy a new coat, although she knew it wasn't in the budget. She needed permission from Jim. She became seductive with him, implying that if she got the coat, they'd have a good time later on.

Jim had gone through this with Josie before. On another occasion, they did what she wanted, and she got her wish, and he was left with his expectation. That evening, Josie got *busy* with the baby and said, "I'll be in, in a little while." The promise of seduction was never carried out.

Jim saw how good she looked in the coat and said, "Yeah, come on. I've heard this before. I know you want the coat. What else are you telling me?"

They both laughed while recognizing that Josie was using her sexuality to get what she wanted. He said, "I don't see how we can afford it."

They left the store and a week later, Jim went back for the coat. It was Josie's Christmas present. Getting your partner a gift that you know he or she will love can be a joyous thing for both of you and the gift needs no strings attached to be joyful for both the giver and the receiver.

The Dovetail Joint

A dovetail is a part or thing shaped like a dove's tail that fits into a corresponding cut-out space to form an interlocking joint. Together the two pieces make a logically connected whole. You and your partner can create that kind of dovetail joint. Marriages that work well create synergism — the simultaneous action of separate entities which, together, have greater total effect than the sum of their individual effects. It's the way our muscles work together to create our movements, or the way the different parts of our bodies work together to make us think, walk, talk, act.

Marriages that work well show the synergistic effect of the whole. Things dovetail; they fit. The fact that we are different makes us work together. You are one circle and I am another. We are two separate identities. Where we overlap and communicate is where our marriage is. In that joining there is a reunion with one another. And every time we are able to reunite with the other person, we experience a reunion with our own selves.

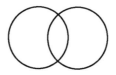

Interdependence of individuals is the only place where we can relate to each other. When we are interdependent, we can depend on one another without necessarily being dependent. We need each other, yet we are individuals. We are able to ask for what we need, give what is needed, and give and accept a "No" answer.

Coming To Your Senses

I like the phrase "coming to your senses." Literally, it means listening, looking, learning again the way you did when you first came into this world — through your five senses. It means forgetting games and myths, putting an end to behavior you've learned to protect yourself. It means seeing, hearing, smelling, tasting, touching and remembering what it's like to experience the world for what it is. It is being yourself and reminding yourself who your self is.

Coming to your senses is an attainable goal, although never an easy task. It requires being able to laugh at the negative nonsense of your unanswerable questions and the pursuit of happiness. Accepting things the way they are is both a way to reduce extraneous suffering and to acknowledge the reality that all problems are not solvable.

The *bigshot* does not feel exceptional about himself; he desperately needs to *appear* exceptional, and he cannot. Exceptional people are the ones who have accepted who they are and who live their lives on that basis. The exceptional person accepts life — right, wrong, good, or bad — as it is. You can do this too.

When we are not okay with ourselves, we start projecting, and pretty soon we have to make our partner as *not okay* as we feel about ourselves. This means actually believing we can make our partner fit our illusions. The more we feel our partner doesn't respect or appreciate us, the more we tend to blame others.

Two Views Where There Once Was One

For some of us, our identity is tied up to a big house, a fancy car, the *right* career. For others, identity means being like our parents, whose teachings we carry into our relationships. Identity for yet others is hooking up with a partner and melting into one.

Two people can pull in the same direction without shutting their individual windows. Seeing through one another's window is the best. If I see through your eyes, I can see the world differently than I have before and therefore have two views of the world — mine and yours. This is expansion — not throwing yourself out. Seeing your partner's perspective does not mean you must accept that perspective for yourself; it means you now see another dimension of the world you never would have seen.

In a paradox, truths that appear to be contradictory do not necessarily cancel or dominate each other. Instead, they stand side by side. If you believe sex three times a week is a lot, and I believe sex three times a week is hardly at all — neither of us is right, and neither of us is wrong. Right and wrong is not what matters. What matters is: Do we want a sexual relationship? If so, what do we do to create mutual happiness?

10

RECONCILIATION

We want the same, but we want it differently.

—The Paradox of Reconciliation

Tourists go to the Grand Canyon, spend half a day, and say, "I've been there; I've seen it." Myself, I can go there 100 times and never totally see it. When you and your partner are in touch, you are also in touch with life around you. You look and feel vital. You feel so good about your own sense of being and value that you begin to see many different facets of nature's wonders.

The same can be true in your relationships. You can be continually fascinated with one another when you see, hear and touch each other with your eyes, ears and minds open.

Don and Betty

Don said, "There's no way I'll be able to tolerate a wife who makes more money than I do." He expected Betty to then agree to lower her income.

Betty said, "Great! I'll never have to worry about only doubling our income. I can count on you to always stretch to triple it!"

Don was stunned by Betty's response, amazed that she would respond the way she did to his attempt to control her. He was astonished that she'd still do her best for herself. He moved from being controlling to seeing Betty as one of the natural wonders of the world.

Reconciling is rejoicing in the rewarding aspects of each other's individuality. It is renewing your decisions about your life and your relationships with those near and dear. Whether the decision is to divorce or to stay together, reconciliation is a coming together to agree on a plan of action. This is why this reconciliation must be based on truth.

One of the major reasons for separation and divorce is that at least one partner in the relationship is emerging with a *real* agenda. Whether you are renewing your relationship or ending it, why not begin relating based on the truth of who you really are? If you are staying together, you can feel that glorious freedom that comes with being your real self and living with someone who is being his or her true self. If you are separating, you can begin your new life as you — that person you ran away from a long time ago.

The Meaning of Reconciliation

Reconciliation begins with being who you are. It is giving up the facade and expectation of being something for someone else or for yourself that you cannot be, and accepting yourself. You and I may disagree, yet when we can accept certain traits in each other, we can accept them in ourselves. If I accept that you have a nasty temper and sometimes need to let out steam, I can accept my own temper and not think less of myself for it.

When we are who we are, we can be honest, direct, serious, funny, energetic, whatever we want with each other. We can speak our hearts and minds, make mistakes, respect one another's opinions, disagree vehemently and still share a spiritual essence. Exciting things can happen between us. If we have to be apart, these feelings of energy, trust, and intimacy can go with us.

The process of healing begins with forgiving yourself for any self-imposed blame and looking at the absurdity of having blamed yourself. We can say, "I'm not a bad person because of this happening. I did my best and it still happened." When we don't forgive ourselves for what's going on in our lives, we project that blame onto other people. Not forgiving ourselves leaves us feeling that there is still something unfinished, unresolved in ourselves.

Yes, I Love You, and Yes, I'm Leaving

While reconciliation means, "I accept myself, and I accept you for who you are," it can also mean, "There are certain things I cannot accept anymore, and, regrettable as it may be, I am leaving." It's saying, "I accept who you are, nonetheless this part of who you are has a negative effect on me, and it hurts me to see you this way." It's saying, "I cannot change you — you are who you are, and in order for me to be happy, I must live somewhere else."

If we make the decision to stay in a relationship in which there is no hope for reconciliation, that's a choice made to struggle. Reconciliation is believing we have the power to change, to improve our situation, instead of using all our power and energy to stay in a struggle that's totally negative and futile.

Sometimes, reconciliation is leaving bad enough alone and walking away. Such a second order change begins when we start to explore, get out from under the old *shoulds* and do what we haven't done before. This does not mean giving up on Christmas because we find out there is no Santa Claus. It is merely giving up

the propaganda that goes with Christmas —
buying the *right* gifts, practicing good will for a
week, conforming to what other people expect
of us.

Reconciliation is learning how to
distinguish needs from wants. Food, love, shelter,
positive regard and work are needs. Everything
else is a want. It is understanding that each of us
has a little kid inside who has a wish book.

Reconciling means recognizing that
the only person in the world you can change is
you. The road to success is to compete with
yourself, not someone else. Therefore, if your
partner is not ready for change, you can at least
take care of yourself.

Yes, I Love You, and Yes I'm Different

We must talk with each other about
what is real. Then our hidden agendas and
manipulations disappear, and we can enter into
a true partnership. When we reach the point at
which we can celebrate our differences, we can
develop a healthy way of supporting each other
and the relationship.

Most things are reconcilable if we first accept our own differences within ourselves, then accept differences in others. This means:

Owning and re-owning our relationships as our own creation. When you and I first met and found each other compatible, we each had needs that the other satisfied. Whatever our relationship is, we ourselves are responsible.

Rejoicing in the rewarding aspects of one another's individuality. You get angry easily. Yet, I admire your strong sense of justice.

Re-deciding how to live our lives and enjoy our relationship. What can we do to make us both happy?

Re-building our relationship or dissolving it. Can we commit to working through our problems together? Do we need to work through them separately?

There's a great paradox in relating; it comes from wanting the same differently. We are lost if we expect that because we love each other, our perceptions won't ever contradict the other's. Our perceptions and the way we articulate them are always different.

If we don't identify the games and myths that have prevented our reconciliation — and we separate from our partner — we are doomed to repeat the same games in any relationship that follows.

There are ten basic steps to reconciliation. They can be helpful if you take the time and interest to sit down with your partner and discuss them, one step at a time. If you cannot both do this together, it's not going to work.

Ten Steps to Reconciliation

1. **Define the current circumstances.** Take time to sit down and say, "What's going on in our lives right now? Let's do an assessment." Are we satisfied? What's our money situation? Are we content where we're living?

2. **Define the differences between you.** If you do this early in your

relationship, you will more readily accept one another's style and way of being. If you're starting right now, the key is for each of you to own your own life. Reconciliation is accepting that you don't agree and then doing the best you can to resolve the issue.

3. Define the process; don't look for who's at fault. Own *your* responsibility in the relationship. We have a tendency to blame others when we cannot explain or understand or accept ourselves. Reconciliation comes from accepting, with compassion, each other's position in life, without blame.

4. Let go of inappropriate expectations. For a solid relationship, get those romance novels out of your living room and out of your head. They are fantasies. When there are unspoken conditions, both romance and love disappear. What other expectations have you had? Get them out in the open. Talk about them. Laugh about them.

5. Renegotiate your commitment.

Marriage and love need strong, supportive anchors. What we did in the past to support and nurture each other may no longer be working. Each of you make a list called "What I Need To Feel Nurtured By You." Exchange lists; hang them on a bulletin board. Honor them.

6. Confront painful issues without defending yourself.

When bottom lines are clear, we can eliminate unconscious expectations. What painful issues do you need to confront today? Tell your partner, "I feel angry when.... Is there something we can do?"

7. Commit to priorities that are in the best interest of the relationship.

Committing to attainable short-term goals clarifies the priorities that are in the best interest of the family. "Let's work out a budget, so we find out where our money is going." "Let's put aside one or two hours on Saturdays for talking about what's going on with us."

8. Be prepared for breakdowns.

There is no absolute Utopian way. There are always pitfalls, detours. Accept them as a fact of life. "This talk didn't get us anywhere. I feel like we're right where we started. Can we sleep on it tonight and start again tomorrow?" "Don't give up on me. I'm not understanding, and I'd like some time to think this over. When can we talk again?"

9. Do fun things together again.

Remind yourselves of the things you did when you first met. Talk about things you can do together that you both enjoy. Make certain you don't wind up doing what only one person likes and the other is not excited about. Don't give your self up. It could be simply walking on the beach, eating out in a restaurant you both enjoy, going to a movie you both want to see, visiting a museum, playing a game.

10. Work through issues as much as possible together. With a positive attitude, more gets done. If you are

embedded in resentments, you will find it difficult to talk. Air out resentments or problems immediately; lay your cards on the table. If you prefer, you can ask for the assistance of a counselor. This is not always productive. Couples will sometimes hold the counselor responsible for the reconciliation process. If you can work out your differences together — just the two of you —your reconciliation will take a stronger hold.

Acknowledge one another's humanity; be tender and caring. What have you got to lose? Let yourself be vulnerable. Put yourself in the here and now. Rather than punishing yourself and one another for past mistakes, open up your resentments and ask where you can go from here. Allow yourself to receive tenderness from your partner if your partner wants to give it to you. Allow yourself to give tenderness to your partner. Life is too short to live any other way.

The Loss of A Loved One

Reconciling the loss of a loved one is the most difficult reconciliation of all. Our sense of loss is the feeling of being damaged and deprived by having something taken from us. Although harsh and cruel, loss is as much a part of life as gain. Neither loss nor gain can be measured unless you have both. By overcoming losses, we gather our strength and momentum to make gains; as our props and projections disappear, our sense of self becomes prominent. Loss appears to be a taking away, yet it really offers us an opportunity.

I wouldn't be a therapist now if my first wife and I hadn't divorced. We can take advantage of every situation; we just need to look at what's available. When people separate and leave a marriage, and allow themselves time to be by themselves, with themselves and to live for themselves, they become very strong — stronger than they were in the marriage.

The illusions of romance become apparent in the attempts of some newly divorced people to quickly reorganize, socialize, show independence and get reinvolved, when a great deal is still unfinished emotionally. If you jump out of one relationship directly into the next one, you're going to rob yourself of knowing your self.

There are qualities that can be re-deemed even though they might appear to have been lost. I always look for the one strength or the one quality that I can see and use humor, to warm it, soften it, assure it, dignify it:

> "My God, you went out and got a job *already*, and he just left you?"

> "You're taking your kid to the show Saturday, *all by yourself*? How are you going to manage that?"

When people feel warmth and car-ing, they immediately sense trust and joy. That's when they start to look at themselves and say, "I put up with him for 15 years!" The loss begins to look humorous; the reasons appear ridiculous. It's a great opportunity to sit down and get feed-back from one another on what this is all about and where it fits in your lives. Going through this allows us growing time, time for the people we had put on the back burner. We can get back to basics with people.

When you have something of value taken away, you must replace it with something of value. Look for the blessings your loss has given you; they will get your through some rough times. "One door doesn't close that another doesn't open."

The Paradox of Problem-Solving

Ain't it awful? Why me? How did I fail? Where did we go wrong? If only I would have... If only I could have... No one understands me. What will I do now? Poor me. I'll never make it.

These are not statements and questions that lead to solving problems. They are utterances of self-pity and self-blame.

We can look at the problem or we can look at the solution; the content is the same. The only difference is our attitude toward the situation.

What has been lost is the same as what is left: love, self-respect, ability to love again, capability of functioning, parenting dignity, spiritual essence. Reconciliation is accepting loss, acknowledging that whatever happened, happened, and that you did your best. It is contacting the essence of the other human being and coming to closure with dignity and respect for each other, instead of re-chewing the bitter stuff that is long gone that nobody can do anything about.

Joe and Andrea

Joe and Andrea constantly clarify whether a situation is okay with the other or not. After dinner Andrea likes to talk about her work day. Joe listens. Then he wants to go watch football. He asks if it's okay with her. No resentment? Am I going to hear about this afterward? His not wanting to hear every detail of her work day becomes okay with her, because she has the option of saying she's not finished yet and wants his company longer. Knowing she has this option, she's more willing to say, "Yes, off you go; we're okay." They both win: She feels heard; he gets to watch football.

We all need to appraise our lives at times and look into our needs and wants. Marriages need to be appraised: What is this marriage about? Where do we get support? How is it used? If we want positive aspects supported, we need to be clean, straight, honest about what's going on with us as people. It takes some effort to make an assessment of what's in our interest and what isn't.

Wanting The Same, Differently

We are all very much alike; we just express ourselves differently. We all have need for love, understanding, trust, health, companionship, housing, food, all the essentials of life. The ways we express our needs and satisfy them are what's different. Things run amok when we believe we need to express ourselves in the same way, without differences.

Person A Believes He Is 100% Right

\+

Person B Believes She Is 100% Right

= Divorce

There is truth in both your belief and my belief. If we disagree, we see one another's belief as contradictory. In fact, they are contradictory only because we see them that way. Two other people with the exact same beliefs might not find them contradictory.

The Well Placed Word

Seven-year-old Billy was tired, angry and confused; he was crying and said, "You don't understand me, Dad." His father said, "Help me."

Billy's father could have offered many different responses. He could have said, "Sure, I understand, kid. This is what's going on, damn it; let me explain it to you." He could have said, "I don't have time for this! Go to bed!" Instead, he made contact.

Being direct and honest with well-placed words help develop contact so the other person doesn't get angry or hurt. Without contact, we have no communication and we have to deal with our feelings of anger and hurt instead of what the communication is about.

Differences Make For Growth

In our urgency to take the most we can from an uncaring and impersonal world, we lose our ability to accept and appreciate differences. Differences are perceived as threats when, in reality, they are the source of challenge and change and a gauge by which growth can be measured. There is no easy way to accept differences until we accept our own differences as they relate to someone else's.

We have to get together and make an agreement to approach the issues that are not sitting right with us. We have to agree to confront one another about whatever is going on without that confrontation meaning the end of the relationship. It means that we are important enough to one another to keep things clear between us, to take care of what needs caring.

Search for Proper Therapy

If the decision is to go into therapy, there is a chance for reconciliation of the marriage if both partners come into therapy together. If only one partner goes into therapy, whatever trust is left could be snapped.

Approach involvement with therapy as a consumer researching the purchase of a product. Beware of red tag sales and "I can handle any kind of problems you have." Beware of those who are too accommodating financially, for they are not very busy. Those who cover too many areas of conflict and pain will not be helpful to your specific and important needs. Question the therapist who is not willing to ask for consultations when there appears to be a breakdown in progress. Take very good care of yourself in this endeavor.

Reconciliation can be done by individuals outside the therapy situation, at home. When both partners are willing to respect one another's differences and confront issues in a non-attack way, and keep a vision of what is in the best interests of the relationship, miracles can happen.

My office is merely for practice. The real reconciliation takes place in your day-to-day life.

11

THE SPIRITUAL SELF

Having spiritual contact
with someone you love
is reliant upon the
acceptance of your real
self and the real self of
the other person.

—The Paradox of Spiritual Contact

Somewhere in our lives, we must
make the decision that we are not better or
worse, above or below others — rather, that we
and they have something — our humanity, our
essence, our spirituality, our way of being — in
common. Reconciliation is looking at what we

are as human beings — how we are connected
to some spiritual essence and force in the world
— and realizing that there isn't much difference
between any of us at any given time on any
given day in our lives.

Integration of Mind and Feelings

When we integrate mind and feel-
ings, we become one with our essence. We become the one we're supposed to be. When we
reconcile mind and feelings, there's a fascination
with life — a celebration of ourselves in the world.

The final reconciliation — the ulti-
mate grace and way to win — is to say, "I did the
very best I could with what I had at the time this
situation was going on. And so did everybody
else in the situation. That's all we had." The day
you forgive yourself and your partner is the day
you begin to live your own life. How strong are
our needs for acceptance and approval and yet
we remove all chances to attain them as we
struggle to escape the ultimate truth — our
selves.

The Paradox of Human Behavior

Much of what we do as human

beings is ridiculous, considering the short time we have on this earth. It's absurd that what we're looking for is the good life and what we end up with is the dregs, because we squeeze too hard.

When we forget to have fun in our relationships, life gets serious, washed out, worn out, dragged out, talked out, beat out because nobody's quite satisfied with what they're getting. Fun is the soil that nurtures the relationship. I like to think of it as *soft thinking*. Humor lightens the control issues and shows the absurdity of attempting to manipulate, control or be powerful over someone else.

A healthy, enjoyable way to look at the differences between you and your partner is to do it with humor. When you're in for the win, the kill, there's no way you will be humorous. The choice to make each other as miserable as possible is an absurd way to spend a life.

Karen and Alan

Alan is a no-nonsense, aloof, straightforward man who loves his privacy and going fishing. He is married to Karen, a gracious, well-bred, outgoing woman. Their different personalities leave lots of room for differences. They agree, however, on a tradition. On their anniversary, they go out to dinner at an elegant restaurant and toast one another with the best champagne.

Recently Alan returned from a fishing trip on the day of their anniversary. Karen could tell he had forgotten what day it was. She got a mischievous look in her eye and said, "Let's go out for dinner tonight." They agreed on a place. That night, Karen ordered champagne. When it was poured, she said, "Let's drink a toast." Alan said, "To what?" Karen said, "To our anniversary."

Alan was surprised, momentarily embarrassed that he had forgotten, and ultimately relieved that Karen had created a positive situation out of what could have turned into pouting, feeling let down, blaming and arguing.

Karen is the kind of person who makes the most out of her marriage.

She finds a resolution to conflict
before the conflict ever has a
chance to begin.

Practicing Humor

Here are some situations you and
your partner can talk about together to practice
looking at your relationship under the soft light of
humor. As you examine each situation, ask one
another:

How would you handle this situation?

What would you say?

What would you do?

Does something about this situation
frighten you?

Is there a way we can have fun with
this and feel satisfied?

The Big Bill

You are paying bills and you come
across a large bill from Saks Fifth
Avenue. Your partner has spent a
chunk of money on clothing — and
it's not for you.

A Night At The Opera

Your partner has tickets for the opera, and there's no way in the world you are going to spend an evening at the opera.

The Birthday Trip

Your partner is an avid bicyclist and has planned a 400-mile bicycle trip that happens to fall right on your birthday.

Couch Potato vs. Gad-About-Town

You have your own business and spend your work day at home staring at a computer. Your partner is on the road every day and thrilled to get home at night and stay there. You want to go out for dinner, see a movie, go for a walk; your partner wants to curl up on the couch, watch a TV movie, read a book.

You know what the differences are between you and your partner — the ones that cause disagreements, bad feelings, fights. Take one of the situations you deal with on a day-to-day basis and treat it like the ones above. Ask one another the same questions. Find a way to treat your differences that bring you to a resolution — within yourself and with your partner.

What you need the most is usually what you're the most afraid of. What you're most afraid of is what you deny yourself the most, which is why you need it so much!

In adult relationships, where healing love is available, we sometimes shy away from it. If our belief about life says that we can't have it, we miss it or reject it when it comes by. When what we want is all around us, we often deny it. When it's taken away, we go after it again. And we still don't get it.

If you have a belief system that says you're not lovable, you could be surrounded by the most beautiful, intense love in the world, and you would deny it because you would be hard pressed to admit that you are lovable. Such an admission would challenge your entire belief system.

Humans are beings with spirits and souls, and we cannot be in a true relationship with others without attending to both their spirit and our spirit. Accepting the reality of self is an essential precondition to a spiritual and energetic contact with those you meet in your life.

We say we are seeking peace, yet peace isn't lost. We forget to express it when we don't accept other's differences, when we demand from others more than what is available, and when we lose our sense of loving and caring.

Children know how to let joy and peace in; they are not as damaged and defensive as we are. They find joy in sitting in a pile of sand, scooping it up with plastic cups into buckets they cart to the beach. We let other people into our lives, not even by cupfuls — by thimblefuls — especially the people we say are nearest and dearest to us. Joy comes from getting to know one another intimately. Peace comes from working through whatever hurt there is. Love is the end result — and life doesn't care how much love you scoop into your bucket.

Arnold Wallace, Ph.D. is the founder and director of A. Wallace and Associates, Inc., a rehabilitation firm in Solvang, California. He is a licensed Marriage and Family Therapist specializing in alcohol and drug abuse treatment and is a member of the California Association of Marriage and Family Therapists. Dr. Wallace holds a Ph.D. in Clinical Psychology and has spent the past 26 years in marriage and family counseling in Canada and the United States. He has taught at Antioch University in Santa Barbara, California, and has been a mental health consultant/therapist at the federal prison in Lompoc, California. As a Diplomate of the Gestalt Training Center in San Diego, California, he has trained mental health professionals in Gestalt psychotherapy.

Dr. Wallace's own recovery process from alcoholism, divorce and the loss of a daughter add a compelling and realistic perspective to his approach to the problems that plague the families of America today. His popular book. *Loving Tough, Loving Smart, Loving You,* written for those who live with alcoholics, is based on clinical as well a personal experience.

He currently lives in the Santa Ynez Valley of California with his wife and son.

Adryan Russ has recently moved her editing house from Santa Barbara, California to the Los Angeles area. She holds an M.A. in English from the University of Illinois with minors in psychology and music. Ms. Russ has taught English, both in the U.S. and in South America as a Peace Corps volunteer. Her interviews and articles have been published in several magazines, and she has served as editor for members of the California Association of Marriage and Family Therapists. Ms. Russ has also been assistant to Drs. Jordan and Margaret Paul in their workshops for couples, based on their books *Do I Have To Give Up Me To Be Loved By You?* and *If You Really Loved Me...* Ms. Russ especially enjoyed working with Dr. Wallace on *Loving Tough, Loving Smart, Loving You.*

With her husband, Dale Alan Cooke, she enjoys theater and first edition books.

SUCCESSFULLY DIFFERENT

An Alternative To Divorce

ISBN 0-9625341-1-0

_____copies @ $11.95 per copy, sub-total $_____

Applicable sales tax $_____

Shipping $_____

Total $_____

Book Rate: (allow 3-4 weeks for delivery) $1.50 per book; 90¢ each additional book
First Class: $2.50 per book

Make checks payable to
Challenger Press, P.O. Box 919 G, Solvang, CA 93464

You may return the book(s) within 30 days from the date of delivery for a full refund if you are not satisfied.

Please ship my order to:

NAME_____

ADDRESS_____

CITY _____

STATE/ZIP _____